Cas,
Wishing you " " " "
John "Barry" Cobon

TWENTY-FIVE STRATEGIES FOR ORGANIZATIONAL SUCCESS

JOHN GASTON

WestBow Press
A DIVISION OF THOMAS NELSON & ZONDERVAN

Copyright © 2017 John Gaston.

All rights reserved. No part of this book may be used or reproduced by any means, graphic, electronic, or mechanical, including photocopying, recording, taping or by any information storage retrieval system without the written permission of the author except in the case of brief quotations embodied in critical articles and reviews.

This book is a work of non-fiction. Unless otherwise noted, the author and the publisher make no explicit guarantees as to the accuracy of the information contained in this book and in some cases, names of people and places have been altered to protect their privacy.

WestBow Press books may be ordered through booksellers or by contacting:

WestBow Press
A Division of Thomas Nelson & Zondervan
1663 Liberty Drive
Bloomington, IN 47403
www.westbowpress.com
1 (866) 928-1240

Because of the dynamic nature of the Internet, any web addresses or links contained in this book may have changed since publication and may no longer be valid. The views expressed in this work are solely those of the author and do not necessarily reflect the views of the publisher, and the publisher hereby disclaims any responsibility for them.

Any people depicted in stock imagery provided by Thinkstock are models, and such images are being used for illustrative purposes only. Certain stock imagery © Thinkstock.

ISBN: 978-1-5127-7738-3 (sc)
ISBN: 978-1-5127-7739-0 (hc)
ISBN: 978-1-5127-7737-6 (e)

Library of Congress Control Number: 2017902959

Print information available on the last page.

WestBow Press rev. date: 2/21/2017

For Maybella Jean Gaston
Best Friend, Wife, Mother

CONTENTS

Preface ix
Introduction xi
Strategy 1: Take Care of Yourself 1
Strategy 2: Plan Your Career 11
Strategy 3: Fall in Love with Learning 21
Strategy 4: Take Some Quiet Time. 27
Strategy 5: Practice Time Management 31
Strategy 6: Be a Leader 37
Strategy 7: Create a Positive Work Environment. 51
Strategy 8: Communicate. 59
Strategy 9: Take Care of the Boss 65
Strategy 10: Picking New Leadership-Team Members Wisely . 71
Strategy 11: Taking Care of the People and the Organization . 77
Strategy 12: Staff for a Stable Labor Force 83
Strategy 13: Hire the Veteran 93
Strategy 14: Control Compensation. 97
Strategy 15: Ensure Customer Satisfaction. 103

Strategy 16:	Make Quality a Top Priority	107
Strategy 17:	Establish a Process-Management System	113
Strategy 18:	Engage in Program Management	119
Strategy 19:	Control Overhead	125
Strategy 20:	Protect Proprietary Information	133
Strategy 21:	Use Strategic Planning	143
Strategy 22:	Plan for Contingencies	147
Strategy 23:	Form Business Alliances	151
Strategy 24:	Know the Competition	155
Strategy 25:	Understand Snakes, Alligators, and Weasels	159

Conclusion 165

Glossary 169

About the Author 177

PREFACE

For years, I've wanted to document the hundreds of lessons I've learned from leading and managing some of the most dedicated, multi-disciplined, mission-oriented, customer-focused, quality-driven professional teams one could find in government and industry. They consisted of scientists, engineers, physicists, chemists, psychologists, intelligence analysts, battle-management directors, and special-security specialists. Several of these teams received national recognition for excellence and set the standard for others. I also had the great honor of working for and supporting some of the most phenomenal leaders and managers one could find within several very dynamic communities—scientific and technical intelligence, research and development, tactical intelligence, combat operations, advanced aircraft manufacturing, and programs involving the nation's most sensitive and classified research.

Thanks to these individuals, I was exposed to innumerable government and industrial decision-making discussions, program reviews, and executive-level meetings that impacted multimillion- and multibillion-dollar programs, and involved thousands of workers and hundreds of suppliers. From these leaders, I learned how to create a positive work environment, measure success, fix problems, manage crises, encourage people to excel in whatever job they had, and motivate individuals to think outside the box and push the envelope.

Conversely, I had the misfortune of working for some of the most incompetent, unethical, self-serving, duplicitous, finger-pointing narcissists one could hope to avoid. From these individuals, I developed an understanding of what not to do, what does not work, and how to turn off or alienate the very people who did the work and completed the mission. The twenty-five strategies outlined in this book are based on lessons learned from working for and supporting both groups for forty-plus years and leading some fifteen teams in government and industry. The strategies are based on personal involvement, experience, and observation as a leader, manager, and corporate executive-level officer for a multimillion-dollar company within a multibillion dollar corporation.

The primary goal of this book is to help the reader leapfrog many years of experience with strategies developed and nurtured from doing things that worked and things that failed. My hope is that these principles will position the reader to be more successful as a manager, leader, executive or entrepreneur. Many of the principles are self-explanatory, while others are expanded. My objective was to keep each strategy short, concise, and organized for fast review and quick follow-up reference while reducing repetition. However, since many of the strategies feed in to one another, some duplication is unavoidable. Many of the principles can be quickly and easily integrated into one's leadership and management style with little effort or fanfare.

This book is about our most valuable and critical resource: people, those wonderful, talented beings who can dream, design, create, produce, and fix a myriad of fantastic things that enhance and protect our existence.

INTRODUCTION

As stated in the preface, this book provides information to help the reader leapfrog many years of experience with the help of lessons learned in leading, managing, succeeding, and sometimes coming up short. The following twenty-five strategies outline specific, proven approaches in government and industry that will position the reader to better lead and manage any size or type of organization.

The strategies fall into three basic categories:

1. The first category—strategies 1 through 9 plus strategy 25—centers on you as leader and manager and are more personal in nature. They discuss how critical it is for you to take care of your mental, physical, emotional, and spiritual well-being; plan your future; expand your knowledge; schedule quiet time; and incorporate a time-management routine into your daily and weekly schedule.

2. The second category—strategies 10 through 13—focuses on selecting your leadership team; creating and maintaining a positive work environment; and building a stable workforce.

3. The third category—strategies 14 through 24—delineates strategies for continually raising quality and customer satisfaction; making continuous improvement a mind-set to reduce overhead and non-value-added costs; protecting trade secrets; developing strategies and contingency plans; forming business alliances; and monitoring domestic and foreign competitors.

These strategies are based on my personal observations, involvement, and participation in making leadership and management decisions; providing direction and focus; and measuring organizational performance. The challenge and secret to building a high-performance organization is creating and nurturing a positive, can-do work environment. In each assignment, I have found that professionals will flourish beyond all expectations in such a setting—particularly because they enjoy intellectual challenge, structured flexibility, creative latitude, empowerment, and opportunities to excel.

Each strategy opens with a little background as to the reason behind the strategy. A list of hard-core rules follow, based on numerous real-world experiences. Many of these do not require additional comment, but some are combined with other items of import under key points and are appreciably expanded in the discussion section. The last item is the sidebar, where personal experience and other supporting information is recapped.

The book was designed for quick initial and follow-up review of information relevant to specific requirements. Each strategy offers a great deal of information for those approaching or entering the job market; entering management; moving up the management and executive ladders; and leading a program, business enterprise, or profit center. Most of the principles apply to leading and managing an organization of 10, 100, 1,000, 10,000, or even more individuals. The reader is encouraged to challenge, modify, spin, or expand each tenet to fit his or her style and the needs of the organization or program. While some points are obvious, others are expanded to provide greater insight and understanding.

This book is not a scholarly work that references studies, statistical analyses, in-depth research, or the advice of industry captains. It is one man's take on how to transform a good organization into an outstanding world-class performer.

The term *organization* is used extensively throughout the book to identify any level of organization within a larger enterprise or corporation, such as a department, directorate, division, branch, group, team, or working group.

STRATEGY 1

Take Care of Yourself

You are the most important person in your life. How many times have you heard the phrase "If you don't take care of yourself, how can you take care of others?" As the person most vested in your life, why not take better care of it? If you are in good mental, physical, emotional, and spiritual shape, you are in an excellent position to take on any job or challenge you choose, as well as taking care of the needs and wants of those who depend on you. Strategy 1 is devoted to *you* and the things you can do now to raise yourself to the next level.

Rules

- Make yourself Priority One.
- Conduct periodic self-assessments.
- Maintain a positive attitude.
- Plan and set goals and timelines.
- Keep your options open.
- Fall in love with learning.

Key Points

1. Get into the mind-set of taking care of yourself.
2. Help others.
3. Conduct a self-assessment.

4. Take full advantage of your downtime.
5. Don't be stupid.

Discussion

1. Get into the mind-set of taking care of yourself.

   - It's important to be sensitive to those circumstances in our lives that generate stress and drain our positive energy. As we become more successful in our profession, our level and scope of responsibility increase appreciably; so also can the negative aspects of stress. Insomnia, weight gain, medication abuse, smoking, and excessive alcohol consumption are all stress factors exacerbated by additional stress events or situations. It is only a matter of time before these negative conditions have a damaging impact on your performance, especially when work-related or family stresses come into play.

     Long-term work peaks demand additional energy and clear thinking to preclude personal burnout. Knowing when to back off, take a break, or make changes is critical to avoiding accidents, incorrect guidance or instructions, lack of attention to detail, or a drop in quality and customer satisfaction. Ignorance is not bliss; doing nothing will lead to mistakes, ineffective leadership and management, and ultimately failure.

   - There are hundreds of excellent books providing guidance on how to deal with stress. Following are a few guidelines that also work well:

     o   Add some structure to your workday and week. Identify a specific day and time for staff meetings, program reviews, customer contacts, team-building sessions, continuous-improvement initiatives, walkabouts, and visits to the exercise room or gym for some personal de-stressing.

- Block off a period each day when you shut your door, put your feet up, and let your mind relax. If more desirable or you do not have an office door, go outside. The primary purpose is to allow your mind to relax from all the activities of the day. However, there are times when such activities are so pressing that they do not allow a mental break. In this case, use personal downtimes to revisit various conversations, guidance, resource allocations, customer feedback, etc. Allow your mind and creative juices to flow without interruption.

- Do what you can to face issues and challenges in a positive frame of mind. Not only does it help you, but it also helps those working for you.

- Maintain a friendly approach. An open-door policy builds confidence in your leadership.

- Play nicely with others, even those you do not trust.

- Do organizational walkabouts. Walk the floors, observe, and talk to people at unscheduled intervals.

- Take outdoor walks, as they stimulate your mind and body.

- Bounce ideas, approaches, and decisions off someone you trust who will not publicize your thoughts or plans.

- Unless there is a deadline that requires you to take work home, leave the briefcase, laptop, and work-related materials at the office. Too often, we get into the habit of taking the office and all the little stresses that go with it home, which reduces the amount of downtime we get to regenerate. By leaving work *at* work, we also help our loved ones, as they want, need, and deserve our full attention at the end of the day.

2. Help others.

- Although it is tempting to ask people to keep their family problems at home, today's challenges make this an almost impossible task. Doing what we can to help individuals with such problems will help keep the individuals focused on the requirements of their job. This in turn will hopefully eliminate quality and safety problems that could impact organizational performance and our ability to provide a safe work environment. Adding flexibility to an employee's work schedule or allowing someone to take unscheduled time off can do wonders to improve morale, respect for management, and overall organizational performance.

3. Conduct a self-assessment.

- Assess your own mental, physical, emotional, and spiritual well-being on a regular basis. A good starting point for any self-assessment is to look at where you are today, where you want to be later, and when you want to be there. Identify those things you can start doing now to achieve your ultimate goal:

    o Mental well-being

    - Keep issues simple and more solvable through a combination of positive attitude and constructive resolution.

    - Be attentive to hot buttons that historically raise your blood pressure. This helps in developing countermeasures. Recognize that, while there are many issues over which we have little influence or control, the stress that's generated is still a waste of energy.

    - Make an effort to do the following each day:

        - Like yourself; understand your strengths and limitations.

- Refrain from belittling yourself.
- Be flexible and open to change or new approaches
- Let yourself grow intellectually, professionally, and spiritually.
- Be kind to yourself and others.
- Learn to relax; do things you enjoy.
- Reduce anxiety and stress by forgiving people who hurt you.

  - Become more knowledgeable of mental health indicators that suggest the need for professional help.

o Physical well-being

  - There is no substitute for good health. Just ask those with medical challenges.

  - Eat healthily. So much information is being published today that identifies which foods will do what, which to eat more of, and which to avoid, especially if you have various health issues.

  - Exercise or find a sport that you enjoy doing.

  - Listen to your body and your doctor.

  - Get six or more hours of quality sleep each night. Taking naps is also good for your health (although not during work hours!).

  - Be sensitive to your body's medical indicators that can signal potential physical conditions.

  - Comply with your doctor's instructions and advice or find another doctor. Similar to other sciences, medical science is continually being updated, and finding a more current medical professional may be appropriate.

  - Recognize the side effects of abusing legal drugs, taking illegal drugs, or drinking excessively. Act to reduce alcohol consumption, drug usage, smoking, and overeating before they become an acute problem. Seek help before the need becomes apparent. A good clue that professional help is warranted is when friends and loved ones change the way and frequency they communicate with you.

- Take pride in your personal and professional appearance. It can do wonders for your physical and mental well-being. Reducing excess weight is one of the most beneficial things we can do for ourselves. Once the weight starts coming off, we feel even greater motivation and self-esteem.

o Emotional well-being

- Spend more quality time with those you care about.

- Take a good look at your personal relationships and identify actions you can take to make them better. Is it a matter of being more respectful, kinder or more attentive? Could you be more flexible or willing to compromise?

- Do you invite your family's input in your personal and professional plans?

o Spiritual well-being

- For those who practice it, religion provides a positive life-enhancing experience that strengthens state of mind, relationships, and value system.

- Spiritual practices offer a sense of fulfillment that can reduce life's many stresses. They provide inner strength and calm that help individuals get through the most difficult, challenging, and significant emotional events.

- Religion provides a framework for moral behavior and decision-making. It helps to put various challenges into an ethical context so as to determine the right or wrong approach to resolving a problem or personal issue. It allows us to operate at a higher level of principled behavior.

- For individuals who were raised in a religious environment, a break in participation can produce an emotional void. Religious involvement often provides a haven during tough times at work or within the family.

- Religion can fill a void for those seeking inner peace. It offers a clear alternative to all the negativity and pain in the world today.

- Trying out or returning to religious participation can help us rediscover and expand the good within ourselves. For Christians, reading the Bible to rekindle our knowledge of its core message can help rebuild our spiritual well-being.

- For those individuals who were never exposed to a positive religious experience, numerous opportunities exist today in local churches, synagogues, TV, and the internet. Initiating communications with a minister, priest, or rabbi may lead to a very positive and enjoyable intellectual journey.

4. Take full advantage of your downtime.

- Whether you prefer physical activities, such as hiking, biking, or running; intellectually stimulating lectures or art exhibits; or pursuits to satisfy your emotional or spiritual wellbeing, opportunities abound. Helping others grow mentally, emotionally, physically and spiritually provides us with a tremendous sense of accomplishment and self-worth.

5. Don't be stupid.

    - No one knows your current mental, physical, emotional, and spiritual state better than you. However, there may be issues that others can see more clearly. Similar observations made by multiple colleagues and loved ones offer a strong indicator that action is warranted. Why not fix those things in your life that require attention? If you need professional help, seek it. If you need support from loved ones, ask for it. The bottom line is to get off dead center and do something about it. No one is saying it will be easy. However, if everyone is noticing a problem, it's time to address it. Don't be stupid. The longer you delay, the harder it will be and the longer it will take to return to your 100 percent level. Make small changes, celebrate your successes, and move on to the next thing. Start today.

Checklist

- ✓ Have you accomplished a personal assessment?
- ✓ Are you where you want to be in your professional life?
- ✓ Are you on track to achieve your personal goals?
- ✓ What is holding you back?
- ✓ Have you asked your family/friends to assess your overall well-being?
- ✓ Have you prepared a plan and timeline to improve any shortfalls?

> This strategy is focused on you, on us. We are the ones who set the tone for quality products and service. We are the ones who push the envelope for innovation, ethical conduct, professionalism, teamwork, and superb customer satisfaction. It is up to us to pull everything together and make it work. We are also the ones who must take action against those whose behavior is either unethical or unprofessional.

It is, therefore, critical that we keep ourselves in good mental, physical, emotional, and spiritual shape so that we can provide the leadership necessary to take the organization to the next level of performance and turn it into a world-class operation.

Too many times I have seen individuals with great potential and promise bypassed for promotion or more responsible assignments because of their unwillingness to resolve personal challenges. Such decisions should represent a wake-up call for repositioning ourselves for the future by eliminating personal distractions.

STRATEGY 2

Plan Your Career

Although it may appear to be academic, career planning can substantially reduce the time it takes to get you from where you are today to where you want to be, and when you want to be there. Planning should include training requirements, possible contingencies, and circumstances involving your loved ones. Planning can be a simple process that involves documenting your goals, timelines and other details as far out as you wish.

Rules

- Make your dream a reality.
- Select a career that you like and want to be part of.
- Develop a timeline.
- Build in flexibility.
- Be willing to regroup or change direction if circumstances warrant.

Key Points

1. Start anytime.
2. Consider the past.
3. Plan for contingencies.
4. Add structure, direction, and focus through planning.

Discussion

1. Start anytime.

   No matter where you are in your career (i.e., just starting out, midway, or in the final phase), you can implement plans for change anytime to help you reach your ultimate goal on your own timetable. Simply thinking about the whats, wheres, and whens of your career can do wonders. Taking action at the earliest opportunity will go a long way in making your life choices more enjoyable and rewarding.

2. Consider the past.

   Do you remember the first time your parents, school counselor, teacher, or coach asked you what you wanted to do with your life? Do you remember your answer? Are you doing what you said? Most people are not. However, are you happy with what you *are* doing, or are you still searching for that right job or career? Has work gotten more complicated? Perhaps it is time to reboot your career.

   Most individuals do remember their first-job answers. Unlike the seventies, eighties, or even nineties, today many persons choose to follow a second, third, or even fourth career path for personal or professional reasons. Sometimes our decisions are hastened by upsurges or downturns in the economy. Some folks undergo a significant emotional event, such as an organizational restructuring. Other times, decisions are driven by disappointment or frustration with the overall situation we find ourselves in.

   How many times have we read stories about people who leave a very high-paying job to do something entirely different with less compensation? How many times have we thought about doing the same? How many times have we heard about individuals who failed not once but several times, only to pick themselves up and keep moving forward?

Waking up every morning and going to a job you thoroughly enjoy is a remarkable feeling. It gives you the sense that you can take on the problems of the world. Whether it is the support of your boss, the organizational culture, or just good people that make the job so enjoyable, it is something you should appreciate, learn from, and not take for granted.

3. Plan for contingencies.

Planning for every career contingency is a new norm, as nothing is certain. Factories moving overseas, businesses closing, and organizations downsizing have all become commonplace. Global corporations have little compassion or sense of responsibility when shutting down plants to reduce labor costs. An awareness of outside influences can make our planning more effective, as we get as many of our ducks in a row as we can, as soon as possible.

The desire for cheaper labor and greater profits has motivated businesses to move various operations to new locations. Foreign competition using cheap labor will continue to undermine US labor rates. Technology is also reducing touch labor as well as man-in-the-middle work environments. Even Wall Street personnel are being replaced by proprietary computer trading. Surprisingly, there are domestic companies whose mission is to convince US companies to move overseas for greater profits.

If past years are any indication, your dream job could end in a heartbeat because of an executive decision made somewhere in the world by people who have little concern for your well-being or happiness. Global organizations can do great things, but we must not be naïve to the fact that profit drives many of their decisions. Having a contingency plan in place minimizes the impact of the sudden loss of one or more jobs. The plan doesn't need to be carved in stone, but periodic discussions with loved ones and reaching a consensus could help everyone get through an otherwise difficult period.

A good human resources department will have information on what organizational and state benefits are available because of downsizings and closings. Research on local and federal programs designed to reduce the impact of such events will also provide options. Keep a file of this information and a current resume handy. Some people have no other alternative but to stay with a troubled organization; however, other options that warrant review and discussion are available. Maintaining contacts within your professional network may produce job offers well in advance of any organizational announcements and could facilitate a much smoother transition.

A little preparation allows you to respond more quickly to job situations over which you have little or no control. Pre-planning can save time, energy, and money while reducing stress and the potential impact of any near-term or long-term economic disruption to the household. However, no matter how much advance preparation you do, other contingencies or situations can affect an otherwise well-thought-out plan—including an unanticipated promotion, reassignment, relocation, sickness, or even death of a loved one.

4. Add structure, direction, and focus through planning.

- Phase One: Initial

    Self-evaluation—Answer the following questions to narrow down your desires, which allows you to focus more time and resources on those jobs that match your desires:

    o   What types of jobs are you good at and happy doing? Finance? Engineering? Computer programming? Security? Art/graphics? Teaching? Electronics? Research?
    o   What are your strengths? Communicating? Problem-solving? Creativity? Logic?
    o   What job category do you want to pursue? Do you enjoy manual labor, or do you prefer using your knowledge to solve problems?

- Do you prefer working with and motivating people in a group situation or working relatively undisturbed on a computer?
- Do you enjoy working outdoors more than indoors?
- Do you enjoy work-related travel? Would you rather stay at or close to home?
- Would you prefer to work for a small organization or a larger, more structured and disciplined one, such as a major corporation or the military?
- Do you want to work in a metropolitan area or smaller city or town?

Timetable—You have chosen a career path. Now determine the following:

- How long do you want to do it? Our parents and grandparents may have been able to retire from the same company or job as when they first entered the workforce, but the probability of that happening today is near zero.
- Do you plan to enjoy this job until something better comes along, or can you see yourself in this position or career until retirement?
- Is this vocation dependent primarily on physical or mental capabilities, or a combination of skills or abilities?

Education and training requirements: To move forward with what you have decided, ask yourself the following questions:

- What are the educational or training requirements for your chosen career?
- Do you need an advanced degree or a technical training degree or certificate?
- Are tests required to determine the aptitude for such a career or job?
- Is a professional certification or license necessary?
- Is an internship required?
- Can you use life experiences, work history, or other training to satisfy established requirements?

Costs—Consider the following financial questions:

o   Do you have the funds available to pay for any education or training requirements?
o   Are no-cost outside resources obtainable, such as scholarships, grants, or co-op programs?
o   Does your current employer support various reimbursable off-duty or after-hours education programs?
o   Does the state offer funds-for-service after certification or graduation, such as teaching?

Getting hired: What must you do to be hired? While there are lots of good people and organizations available to assist you in getting employed, keep the door open for other entry opportunities. You might consider part-time positions, first- and second-tier contractor positions, recruiter advertisements, and even friend-of-a-friend back-door openings.

- Phase Two: Stay the Course or Midway Correction

Self-evaluation—Now that you have been in the workforce for several years, ask yourself the following:

o   Are you happy with your chosen career path?
o   Do you enjoy working for your boss? Are there any issues with leadership style?
o   Is the boss supportive of your career goals? Has management suggested vocation-enhancement courses?
o   Has your boss encouraged a move into management? Is that something you would consider?
o   Are you competitive for a promotion in your current job?
o   Have you taken advantage of upward-mobility opportunities or other internal assignments?
o   How much longer do you want to do your current job?
o   If you are looking, is it a matter of compensation?
o   Do you want to stay within the same organization? Are there new opportunities in a different career field you would like to explore?

- Is there writing on the wall regarding your position or unrest in the organization that management refuses to acknowledge?
- Is it time to leave? If so, it is much wiser to have a job offer before resigning from your current position.

Timetable—Ask these questions to determine how urgently you need to make a change:

- Are you content in your professional life?
- Have you reached the organizational and compensation level you want at this point in your life?
- Is your work located in the geographical area that you like?
- Where are you in regard to accomplishing your personal and professional goals?
- Is it time to modify current goals or set new goals and timetables?

Flexibility—Ask yourself the following questions to determine how much leeway you have in making a change:

- How flexible are you in taking advantage of opportunities as they pop up?
- Does the organization have a positive record for announcing new assignments that carry greater opportunity for upward mobility?
- Are you mentally, physically, and financially prepared to take on a new position elsewhere in the organization on short notice, even if it is in another geographical location?

Other considerations: Whatever new goals or decisions you consider, they must include the needs and goals of your family. Ask yourself the following questions, if applicable:

- What impact will your decisions have on other family members? Many statistics show that in the majority of US households, both parents work. Further, both parents may have professional credentials with corresponding compensation packages that could cause a major disruption. Could the family sustain a short-term separate living arrangement?

o What will the economic impact of the move be? Unless funds are set aside, any change in a job, job location, or career path will have a monetary impact. While some organizations are very generous in their relocation packages, others are not so giving. You may need to absorb some or all non- reimbursed moving costs. Most organizations understand the costs associated with hiring an outsider versus moving a current team member. Therefore, a plan to minimize such impact will reduce stress while ensuring a smoother transition.

- Phase Three: New Opportunities

Take time to determine what you want to do, when you want to do it, and where you want to be. If possible, identify the compensation level for each stage. The same type of mind-mapping can also apply to formal education, technical training, and on-the-job certifications.

Whatever you decide to do, try not to burn any bridges with the current organization, as new opportunities could dry up for reasons no one can anticipate. Although it is courteous to tell your boss you will be leaving the organization for a new opportunity, anticipate changes the company may make to accommodate your departure. Some could be uncomfortable. It may be wiser to keep any departure plans close to the vest until you reach the two-week official notification.

Having a number-two person in place will make any transition much smoother for everyone. Do not feel responsible if the organization elects not to promptly identify a replacement.

Lastly, it is always wise to maintain a friendly relationship with your previous bosses, as it might take some time for them to realize your value. Such a realization could lead to something bigger in the future.

Checklist:

- ✓ Does your career path plan include a timeline, position level, compensation band, and location?
- ✓ Do personal plans incorporate responses to possible contingencies?
- ✓ Do you have an updated contact list for various industry networks?
- ✓ Does your résumé need updating?
- ✓ Do your traveling documents include a résumé?

> There is nothing more rewarding than working in a job you enjoy and being paid a competitive wage. However, it is wise and prudent to think about and plan for various situations that could affect you and your job—and how you would respond. Periodically, discuss your thoughts and plans with your family and loved ones, as it can generate new ideas, approaches, and potential challenges. A word of caution: Do not discuss such plans with colleagues, as they may be used against you when personnel reductions are considered.
>
> While I was working in the defense industry, my organization was required to conduct a reduction in force (RIF) because of a large defense contract cancellation. As a department head, I had to select individuals based on current and projected business requirements and the skills needed to accomplish those requirements. During the following weeks, it became apparent that those individuals who had anticipated such work scenarios were more prepared, thus making their transition easier.

STRATEGY 3

Fall in Love with Learning

Nothing is more gratifying than being identified as an expert in your chosen career field. To be the go-to person for questions and guidance is an overwhelmingly positive feeling. As most career fields are continually advancing, so should we. We should take advantage of every opportunity to expand our job knowledge and our awareness of additional disciplines that can help us grow both individually and professionally. Learning new skills in leadership, management, decision-making, process management, operations, planning, and communications will make us more competitive for new, challenging assignments and upward mobility.

Rules

- Fall in love with learning.
- Knowledge is power.
- Sharing one's knowledge is critical to organizational success.

Key Points:

1. Knowledge is power.
2. Knowledge is essential for personal and professional growth.
3. Conduct a personal evaluation.
4. Develop a plan.

5. Take advantage of organizational subject-matter experts (SME) and leadership-team members.
6. Take advantage of loved ones' knowledge and lessons learned.
7. Take advantage of downtime and travel time.
8. Orchestrate a "Learning Love-In" for the organization.
9. Support outside educational events and programs.

Discussion

1. Knowledge is power.

   Knowledge is one of the few things that cannot be taken from us. We can use the power of knowledge to grow personally and professionally in whatever discipline we wish to pursue. Falling in love with learning early in life will pay tremendous dividends. We can have a dramatic influence on those we care for by helping them grow intellectually, emotionally, and spiritually. The more informed we are, the more successful we can become.

   No matter how many degrees, professional certifications, or licenses we have, we should never stop learning or taking advantage of educational events or opportunities to expand our level of knowledge, skills, and technical expertise. Doing so not only makes us more effective in our current position but also more competitive for positions that are more responsible. Further, it allows us to branch out into other career paths—for example, going from a technical role to management or leadership positions. In our technological age, we can acquire knowledge from numerous sources. Free educational applications are offered daily. It is just a matter of clicking the right buttons.

2. Knowledge is essential for personal and professional growth.

   Whether we function in leadership, management, or a support capacity, using our experience and technical expertise to move the organization to the next performance level will open doors we never knew existed. Unlike the government, big business recognizes unparalleled performance much faster and rewards it more graciously.

3. Conduct a personal evaluation.

   It is very easy to compare your current educational background with the requirements for most positions. Shortfalls in required coursework need to be completed or a written waiver acquired prior to any application. Discuss unwritten requirements with the boss, human resources, or more tenured individuals.

4. Develop a plan.

   Upon reviewing the organization's process for participation, form a plan that outlines a timetable for accomplishing all required training for the job. Include applicable advanced and auxiliary training courses, followed by leadership, management, and communication studies. The plan should also incorporate any payback requirements.

5. Take advantage of organizational subject-matter experts (SME) and leadership-team members.

   Get to know organizational SMEs and leadership-team members when the opportunity arises during on- and off-campus events and travel. Many such individuals enjoy sharing their experiences, lessons learned, and wisdom. Ask them about their biggest challenge or greatest achievement; the answers may surprise you. Likewise, be prepared to respond to their questions regarding your own personal goals.

6. Take advantage of loved ones' knowledge and lessons learned.

   Parents, grandparents, and other loved ones can be valuable resources for job-related and other knowledge. Through their work and life events, they have experienced the value of ethics, communication, work environment, fair pay, and so many other subject areas that affect us in our profession–even though they may know very little of what our particular job entails.

7. Take advantage of downtime and travel time.

    There are innumerable audiovisual products and applications on the market—by renowned SMEs—that can be enjoyed during downtime, during business travel, or while driving to and from work. Another way to use downtime is to coach yourself to be more aware of your surroundings and of people's eye movements, handshakes, or body language, to name a few examples.

8. Orchestrate a "Learning Love-In" for the organization.

    You can coordinate a series of table discussions featuring organizational SMEs from all disciplines—who can discuss their experiences, successes, failures, and lessons learned—in addition to training programs and internal/external training opportunities. Encourage the organization's young and less-experienced professionals to bombard theses SMEs with questions. Schedule such discussions during the lunch period or at the beginning of the duty day. This activity represents a vast information transfer that ultimately benefits everyone.

9. Support outside educational events and programs.

    Colleges and universities offer classes, seminars, and lectures specifically structured to support the changing demands of business. Professional societies frequently fund workshops to focus on new approaches to current/old challenges; additionally, government agencies hold conferences that provide information and seek input regarding policies, regulations, and processes. Organizational support and participation allow us to hear how others are tackling various challenges, while participation as a speaker enables us to share lessons learned and novel approaches to solving challenges. It also provides an opportunity to give back to the community and help others learn from our successes and mistakes.

Checklist

✓ Have we taken advantage of programs to grow our knowledge and skill sets?
✓ Are educational policies and programs for internal and external training opportunities clearly visible throughout the organization?
✓ Does the process for participation clearly identify the requirements and ground rules for participation and any *payback* regarding obligations and refund should the participant terminate their employment?
✓ Does the Leadership Team actively support individual participation?
✓ Is flextime available for individual members with management support?

Very few things compare with becoming a subject matter expert in your job and chosen career field. Not only is it personally gratifying, it represents a powerful tool in helping others achieve their goals and those of the organization to be world-class. Knowledge is power, and using it to grow others will benefit everyone.

As leaders, we must identify and grow those individuals who also share their knowledge with others to strengthen the organization. Encouraging such individuals to acquire more training in their specialty as well as management will appreciably benefit the organization. Giving these individuals greater responsibility will build a stronger management team.

Conversely, we must be aware of those individuals who use information and knowledge as a control mechanism to help solidify their own position, frequently at the costs of others. These individuals foster a *yes* mentality that kills opposing views, ideas, and out-of-the-box thinking. Although these individuals are politically astute, they should not be selected for senior management and leadership positions.

STRATEGY 4

Take Some Quiet Time

Quiet time can do and be many things, but the goal is to allow the mind to relax from the stresses of the day, even for a short period. Leaving the office, going outside, or just closing the door may accomplish this goal. In a fast-paced, high-octane organization, a quiet-time period also provides an opportunity to think, brainstorm, pull back, or regroup. It offers time to plan as well as revisit various decisions, judgments, approaches, or resource allocations. We can also use quiet time as a value-added occasion to look at the "big picture" and head off any budding problems.

Rules

- Schedule a quiet-time period each day, preferably the same time.
- Shut the door and turn off the phone.
- Relax, sit back, and think, plan, strategize.

Key Points

1. Give yourself a break.
2. Quiet time is extremely beneficial.

Discussion

1. Give yourself a break.

   As briefly mentioned in Strategy 1, block off a period each day for some quiet time, preferably the same time each day. Turn off the phone, put a "not now" sign on the door, find a comfortable chair, put your feet up, and just relax. Let your mind and body refocus on things that are important without the bunk. Some individuals may prefer to leave the office, take a walk, and breathe in fresh air. Quiet-time breaks are more critical when things are chaotic, the stress level is overflowing, and deadlines are in a mach mode. Allow your brain to back off a little and look at the big picture.

2. Quiet time is extremely beneficial.

   Sit back, relax, and if desired, mentally go through the day's planned and unplanned activities for various decisions to ensure that tasks, resources, and priorities are in order and need no readjustment or intervention. Consider the following:

   - Is it time to reprioritize tasks and tweak resources?
   - Are there any indications of personnel burnout?
   - Are there resources that can be applied or reassigned?
   - Are minor issues getting too much attention while bigger, more critical, more costly issues are not receiving the attention or resources they require?
   - Is it time to pull in resources from another organization?
   - Are the right people with the right skill sets working the problem?
   - Is there a leadership or management problem?
   - Are there any assumptions that could be in error or may need validation?
   - Are there any self-imposed due dates that need modification?
   - Is there a chance that customer instructions or a senior-management tasking may have been misinterpreted?
   - Is it time to stop an operation and have everyone back off, take a breath, and reengage?

We can revisit the following events of the day for positive or negative fallout, caution lights, lessons learned, a new approach, or the need for follow-up discussions or clarification:

- meetings with the boss or direct reports
- meetings with other organizational heads
- talks with customers
- attending program reviews
- taking walkabouts
- hosting an all-hands meeting
- things that the mind will not let go

Checklist:

✓ Has a quiet time period been established?
✓ Have you discussed quiet time and your ground rules with your administrative assistant or support staff?
✓ What changes should you make?

> Scheduling a quiet period is one of the smartest things we can do for ourselves. It allows us to do more, and all the things stated above. The dividends for the organization and us are unparalleled. It provides us an opportunity to de-stress and look at activities and events in a more positive frame of mind. The need for such quiet time is more critical when the organization is in a high-pitch mode for accomplishing contractual requirements on time, on budget, and as required. I frequently put a sign on my door that simply reads "not now," and it works miracles in allowing me to reduce personal stress and reevaluate many of the factors previously listed for adjustments.

STRATEGY 5

Practice Time Management

Time management offers us a wonderful tool in assessing our day's activities and the amount of energy we expend. It helps us stay in control of our day while reducing stress and non-valued added pursuits.

Within the manufacturing sector, labor costs for product design, prototype fabrication, testing, production, and logistics are all measured in time. In other industries, labor hours are assigned to various campaigns, projects, programs, and customer accounts—all factors that determine ultimate cost and profit margin. Managers are always looking for ways to reduce cycle time to build a product, provide a service, or complete a process.

Simply put, we are all called on to do more in less time. Managers are expected to lead, supervise, coach, motivate, discipline, and reward their team members; prepare reports; attend meetings; give presentations; participate on joint teams; and complete self-improvement training or acquire a higher degree. A time management routine would help!

The following strategy outlines actions that managers can take without enlisting the help of an administrative assistant or support staff.

Rules

- Implement a time-management routine as soon as possible.
- Stick to the routine until you think of something better.

Key Points

1. Time management allows us to do the following:
    - Assume more control of our daily and weekly calendar.
    - Do more tasks in less time.
    - Have more free time.
    - Reduce personal stress.
    - Leave work at work
2. There are several easy, implementable time-management techniques.

Discussion

1. Time management allows us to do the following:
    - **Assume more control of our daily and weekly calendar.** Time management is simply a decision to break up a daily routine into logical segments that benefit our people, the organization, and us. It adds focus and discipline to our workday and is important to implement as soon as possible. Time management produces immediate benefits by reducing the number of non-value hours during the workday. We cannot change our boss' scheduled staff meetings or other organizational meetings that require our presence, but we can control other meetings with our direct reports, all-hands, and customers. We can allocate daily or weekly blocks of time to complete mentoring sessions, paperwork, reports, plans, presentations, customer phone calls, strategy meetings, walkabouts, even quiet time. For example:

- *The best time* to schedule a meeting with direct reports is within a few hours of the boss' staff meeting to transfer information, answer questions, and provide guidance.
- *The best time* to call customers is early, as soon as they become aware of any contract issues. Combining some customer phone calls into a block of time will decrease the number of interruptions later in the day.
- *The best time* to meet with our people is whenever there is significantly positive or negative feedback from customers or from the organization's leadership team. Although it may be disruptive to some, these meetings will head off rumors and incorrect information. Internal electronic communications may also be appropriate, with more in-depth information shared at the next scheduled all-hands.
- *The best time* to have an all-hands is normally Friday afternoon—or whenever a noteworthy event takes place that requires immediate information distribution.

There are many logical reasons to block off time segments for specific tasks while knowing that unscheduled events may periodically preempt them.

- **Do more tasks in less time.** Identifying specific blocks of time daily or weekly to work on a particular task allows us to focus energy, corporate knowledge, and creativity on working that one subject. It also allows us to collect background information and do any additional research on the subject before working it. This simple plan of action allows us to do time-sensitive and routine tasks in less time.
- **Have more free time.** Shortly after implementing a time-management routine, you may realize that you have more time to target those nice-to-do or do-when-time-permits tasks that you had postponed.

- **Reduce personal stress.** Anytime we complete a demanding task, there is a sense of relief, as well as a sense of accomplishment—for example completing a high-value proposal in response to a customer solicitation. Proposal preparation most often involves a cross section of talents, disciplines, and resources across the entire organization. Since such proposals are the lifeblood of many corporations, the stress of submitting a winning proposal represents a true significant emotional event.
- **Leave work at work.** Taking a briefcase or laptop loaded with work makes home an extension of the office. Those items should be left at the office, whether you intend to open them or not. One of the best benefits of good time management is the ability to leave the office at the office. There will be times when you have no choice, but those should be the exception and not the rule.

2. There are several easy, implementable time-management techniques:

- Use relevant time-management software applications for electronic devices.
- If such devices are not allowed in the work center, use an appointment book that provides sections to document staff meeting notes (boss and direct reports), new tasks, customer contacts and discussion topics, lessons learned, scheduling new meetings, personal reminders, "do today" tasks, and observations.
- Combine similar tasks.
- Identify a time block, free of distractions, for writing tasks, proposals, or presentations.
- Identify the best times to host various meetings that accommodate attendee schedules as much as possible.
- Schedule walkabouts.
- Block off thirty minutes or so daily for quiet time to relax, collect thoughts, plan, strategize, identify solutions, revisit

discussions with the boss or customers, or just think of ways to improve overall performance.
- Host working lunches with direct reports to strategize or tackle a recurring challenge.
- Assist program managers by providing a required list of items for program reviews.
- Music is soothing, but travel to and from work is a great time to listen to educational media.
- Business travel is a bonus opportunity to review reports, briefings, and other non-proprietary documents.

Checklist

✓ Have various electronic and paper management tools been reviewed to determine which ones can help the most?
✓ Have personal notes been reviewed for trends or lessons learned?
✓ Have you discussed time-management approaches with peers?
✓ Have various time-management approaches been discussed with direct reports for comments and ideas?

> The sooner we can adjust to a logical, workable time-management routine, the greater the impact on our performance, enjoyment, and overall well-being will be. Once we can start leaving our briefcase or laptop at the office, we will notice a lower stress level and improved quality time with our family. For years, I took a briefcase home thinking I could get ahead of my workload at the time. I finally realized that this practice was counterproductive for my family and for me. It is far better to stay a little longer at the office to finalize tasks than to take work home. We should encourage our direct reports to do the same.

STRATEGY 6

Be a Leader

Whether you are chosen by a committee or promoted from within to assume control of the organization, take charge. Do not assume. Ask those who selected you about their expectations and any specific goals, timelines, or restrictions.

When assuming a new position, let your leadership team know that you are there to lead and work with them in moving the organization to the next level. Let them know that you will challenge all their energies and creative thinking to provide customers with the highest-quality products and services possible. Communicate the vision of making the organization the world-class standard for similar businesses.

Rules

- Lead by example.
- Do walkabouts.
- Talk with your people, listen, and answer questions.
- Set the tone for establishing a positive work environment.
- Set the standard for ethical and professional behavior.
- Never allow discrimination, racism, or sexist behavior.
- Communicate the vision, mission, goals, and performance expectations of the organization.
- Never let personal attacks on your integrity or credibility go unanswered.

Key Points

1. Set the tone.
2. Lead.
3. Set an example.
4. Be a visionary.
5. Be the number-one communicator.
6. Be a recruiter.
7. Reassign poorly performing managers.
8. Nurture the organization's subject-matter experts (SMEs).
9. Make continuous improvement (CI) a way of life.
10. Establish a network of advanced concepts groups (ACG).
11. Do not ...

Discussion

1. Set the tone.

    During the first organizational meeting, introduce yourself and provide a brief summary of your experience. People want to believe that their new leader can effectively run the organization. Without getting too specific, discuss your personal and organizational goals. Do the following to set the right tone:

    - Communicate to people that you are there to lead, to manage, and to run the organization. The proverbial "buck" stops with you. Make sure that everyone fully understands who is in charge and feels encouraged to use the open-door policy to discuss ideas, suggestions, and even complaints.

    - Introduce opportunities to excel in taking the organization to the next level of success and making it world class. Introduce initiatives like a suggestion program or process improvement initiative to help the company become more effective, build higher-quality products, reduce operational costs, increase sales, and expand its customer base.

- Meet individually and collectively with direct reports to discuss their ideas, suggestions, and recurring topics for future meetings. Host working lunches to create relationships, build trust, and enhance communications. Periodic off-campus social events allow everyone to relax and get to know each other on a different level. It also makes it possible to observe various interactions between direct reports.

- Staff meetings should reinforce the need for timely communication regarding any information that may affect one or more of the attendees. It is very desirable to keep the meetings as short as possible, twenty to thirty minutes. Cut off any dragged-on meetings. If necessary, schedule follow-on meetings for topics or issues that require other attendees, such as SMEs. Do not take phone calls during these meetings, use foul language, spread gossip, or criticize the decisions, policies, or official actions of senior management.

- In some environments, such as manufacturing or production, it may be wise to meet daily for ten to fifteen minutes just to talk about issues, problems, status, etc. A fixed agenda for staff and stand-up meetings as new information is received may include:
  o special recognition
  o announcements from higher headquarters
  o emphasis of or changes to organizational policies or processes
  o key personnel assignments
  o current business updates
  o customer announcements or feedback
  o quality issues
  o security and safety issues
  o operational issues (administrative, personnel, finance, facilities)
  o current tasking updates

- o   new tasking
- o   rumor mill
- o   any last-minute pop-ups that require attention

2. Lead.

   Each one of us has the potential to become an exceptional leader. There are thousands of books, hundreds of seminars, and numerous college programs that we can tap into to improve our leadership skills and abilities.

   There are, in essence, two leadership modes within each type of organization, and each depends on the circumstances for selection. A *micromanagement mode* is one in which all information flows through the leader's office where all decisions are decided. Such a mode may be appropriate for an organization having major performance issues, losing contracts, and producing poor-quality products.

   For organizations not in trouble, a *delegation mode* is more appropriate. It includes clear lines of authority, assigned responsibilities, and decision-making. This mode also incorporates a set of measures that highlights successful approaches and decisions as well as potential problems and the need for intervention.

   Whichever mode is implemented, provide your direct reports with some rationale for your approach and offer additional guidelines to avoid confusion and frustration. Ensure that all direct reports know that their input is encouraged but the final decision is yours, and that their support is expected.

   Incorporating the following very simple strategies into my leadership and management styles helped me transform good organizations into nationally recognized awardees by the government customer:

   - Lead, encourage, motivate, mentor, direct, support, provide focus, explain, connect-the-dots, guide, recognize, and build a strong sense of teamwork.

- Closely monitor all performance and operational reporting measures for quality, costs, delivery dates, customer satisfaction, compliance, and security issues for intervention. Once you have discussed the tasking and any progress reporting with your direct reports, back off and let them do their job. Trust your people to have the wisdom to keep you informed of their progress and any pop-up issues. Do not micromanage or intervene unless measures indicate a major problem.

- Maintain a positive attitude. A leader's positive attitude can do wonders for an organization's workforce, especially in down times. Even something as simple as a "Hi, how's your day going?" and a smile makes a difference. Reach out with a "Good job!" and see how quickly a few words or actions boost organizational morale.

- Communicate constantly. Host direct report meetings as often as necessary to ensure a timely flow of communication. We live in the information age, and our people want to know what is going on and why or when there is any change to our plans for accomplishing assignments, missions, and goals.

- Whenever appropriate, connect the dots for your team to illustrate the relationship between teamwork, quality products and services, customer satisfaction, increased business, organizational success, compensation, and job security. There is no substitute for a quality product reputation.

- Be nice and respectful. It allows people to feel at ease and sets the tone for professionalism in all situations.

- Never, ever intentionally mislead or misinform your people. Always be truthful, based on the information you have. Let the people know if the information is incomplete or questionable.

- Never allow attacks on your personal integrity to go unanswered. Your integrity is who you are.

- Delegate, delegate, delegate. Give your direct reports the support and resources necessary to do their jobs and any special assignments. Fully explain budgets, timetables, and expectations. Once you have assigned a specific task, do not allow the individual to move the assignment back to you for whatever reason. Provide additional instructions or guidance and even a new due date, but insist that they accomplish the task. Suggest that it provides them a great opportunity to excel.

- Measure what is important. There is an old saying: "What gets measured gets done." Good measures shed light on successful approaches and potential problems that may require intervention.

- Be aware. Keep your eyes and ears open while attending organizational functions, program reviews, walkabouts, and other events.

- Identify the organization's power brokers. Recognize these people as soon as possible and be sensitive to what they say. Be mindful of those (other than your boss) seeking your insights and opinions upon joining a new organization.

- Be consistent and fair. Although most organizations have well-established policies and procedures, interpretations may vary. Whatever the variation is, be as consistent and fair as possible in providing direction, guidance, praise, or disciplinary action.

- Be creative and constantly look for new ways to challenge the skills, knowledge, and imagination of your people.

- Embrace a continuous improvement mind-set. Encourage everyone to look for better ways to do their job, improve product quality, and provide better customer service.

- Host brainstorming sessions to come up with creative ideas or techniques for solutions to new and old challenges.

- Recognize superior performance or efforts by an individual or a team by making it one of the first items discussed at stand-ups and all-hands meetings. Periodically visit the desk of top performers with an extra cup of coffee, attend a beer call and pick up the tab, visit a new mom in the hospital, send flowers to an employee who has a loved one in a medical facility, or extend leave for someone who has lost a loved one.

- Be your organization's biggest cheerleader. One of your primary responsibilities as a leader is to celebrate, visibly and verbally, both small and large successes. Hosting special and holiday events is appreciated. Motivate, motivate, motivate!

- Be generous. Working within organizational policy, find ways to reward people for going the extra mile. Frequently, it is these and other individuals who spend numerous non-compensated hours completing work that is crucial to the organization's success. Identify and reward such dedication as soon and as often as possible. Granting compensatory or personal time is an excellent way to express appreciation. Extending holiday breaks may increase production before and after the break while reducing the costs of keeping the facility open when most personnel are on leave.

- Allow some flexibility for individuals who need to provide support during unusual family situations. Education and training requirements may also warrant scheduling flexibility. It is vital, however, to maintain a core work period, so this depends on the type of work the individual performs.

- Be your customers' biggest champion. Highlight and monitor any significant customer complaint until the issue is resolved. If possible, communicate directly with the customer.

- Maintain a sense of urgency. No matter what functions the organization performs, a sense of urgency goes a long way in establishing a fantastic reputation for getting things done.

Whether it is producing a new product, servicing a customer's system, or moving products, set timelines to complete specific tasks. Creating a tracking system for major quality issues is just good business.

- When faced with challenges that have no precedent or historical background, use common sense and logic to decide the right approach until more information is available.

- Do not point fingers. When a problem pops up, work on the issue until a solution is identified and implemented. If a get-well plan is appropriate, make sure it identifies corrective actions, milestones, and completion dates. If the issue is personnel-related, a tough-love solution may be in order.

- Remove any key individual who cannot lead or manage. It is critical to the success of the organization to maintain a leadership team that can lead and manage individual functions while supporting each other. In today's highly competitive market, we cannot allow one or more key individuals to cause disruption, distrust, or discord. Once identified, reassign or remove such individuals immediately.

- Never assume. Assumptions generate more problems than necessary. Always, always follow up with any assigned tasks. Too many times an individual with a designated task has no clue or understanding as to how important the job is to a current or parallel task or activity.

- Never allow discrimination, bigotry, racism, or inappropriate sexual behavior or practice. There is no place in any organization in which such behavior can exist. Lewd behavior of any sort is wrong. Once identified and confirmed, the practice must be stopped. Reassign or put on administrative leave any individual accused of sexist or racist behavior until the allegation is investigated. If found to be true, and depending on the nature of the incident, that individual should be disciplined, reassigned, or fired.

- Never allow alcohol or drugs on organizational grounds. Escort anyone identified as under the influence to a medical facility and process for disciplinary or dismissal action in accordance with organizational policy.
- Never criticize your people in public. Correct the problem, not the individual—unless the individual *is* the problem. If so, determine whether the problem is due to lack of training or attitude and requires further action.
- Never allow unethical behavior or practice. This should be a no-brainer, but too many organizations overlook bad behavior if the individual has been with the company a long time and contributed to its success. Simply put, this is wrong. Correct such behavior immediately. The manner of correction should match the behavior. Did the individual understand the policy or practice? A proactive indoctrination and training program will reduce occurrences of this problem.
- Never criticize senior management or their decisions. To discuss decisions is one thing; to openly criticize such decisions is stupid and can shorten one's career with the organization. Senior management may allow many different types of behavior without retribution, but this is not one of them without retribution. It's called "not being a team player."

3. Set an example.

As leaders, we are always in the spotlight for the way we look, the way we communicate, and the way we act and react to positive or negative information. It is most important that we set the example for professionalism, ethical behavior, integrity, mutual respect, fairness, and consistency in working with our people, peers, superiors, and customers.

4. Be a visionary.

It is important that we communicate the vision of the organization and how it supports the vision, mission, and goals of our parent organization. Using existing measurements to discuss where the organization is today will provide everyone with a baseline to create a new focus and direction for reaching new performance goals.

5. Be the number-one communicator.

    We live and work in an age that owes its entire existence to the speed of information transfer. Therefore, it is paramount to disseminate any critical information regarding the organization's business as soon as possible to preclude incorrect or misinformation. Being proactive means letting people know that you are aware of such information and that it is being checked. It is also important to do the following:

    - Periodically communicate the organization's goals to maintain direction and focus.

    - Keep goals simple and easily understood to greatly enhance their acceptance.

    - Use positive and negative performance measures to add credibility and reinforcement. Maximize the use of electronic and paper media to help in this endeavor.

    - An organizational website might be a good communication option, although within a manufacturing organization, paper media and visuals are often more appropriate.

    - Posters and other large paper media products are very effective in reaffirming vision, mission, goals, and performance criteria.

    - Keep policies, operating procedures, government compliance, and other ground rules available for review.

    Additional communication tools include:

    - direct-report and all-hands meetings that encourage Q&A, employee recognition, and a chance to discuss accomplishments, challenges, customer feedback, rumors, and any other hot subject;

- a periodic walkabout to view current activity, talk to people, discuss goals, and answer questions; and
- organization and functions briefings for new personnel and customers.

6. Be a recruiter.

   Continually look for qualified people with a good attitude to join the leadership team. Stay abreast of key management vacancies throughout the organization and ask impressive individuals to apply for consideration. We should also task the human resources team to develop and implement a performance rating system that identifies individuals throughout the organization who demonstrate leadership and management acumen and skills that would make them a candidate for more senior positions.

7. Reassign poorly performing managers.

   Do not hesitate to reassign any management individual—that you hired, promoted, or inherited—based on performance or lack thereof. It is very important to keep less capable individuals from remaining in leadership, technical, or support roles that manage other employees. It is very common for highly technical, highly successful individuals to be selected for leadership and management positions when they have no such skills or desire to learn them. While training can be offered and skills can be taught, changing one's desire may be an unwise stretch. It is much more productive to allow these valuable individuals to return to the job where they flourished and reward their performance in other ways. It is okay to have such individuals make a higher salary than their manager does.

8. Nurture the organization's subject-matter experts (SMEs).

   These critical assets are happiest when they are doing their magic thing, so to speak. Create a work environment that encourages

SMEs to push the envelope, leapfrog current thinking, and go where no SME has gone before. It is wise to have SMEs work in a "think tank" common area, so they can bounce ideas off each other. If circumstances or opportunities allow, SMEs can also function in consultant, trainer, and mentor roles. While some highly technical SMEs flourish in a well-structured setting, others may prefer more latitude and a freethinking environment. The point is to keep an open mind when assigning tasks that will allow these special individuals to think the impossible.

9. Make continuous improvement (CI) a way of life.

    Integrate CI into every facet of the organization's operations, from product design to test and evaluation, to production, to marketing, to sales and service. Continually encourage all individuals to look for better ways to design, build, and service things while performing their functions in the most cost-effective, quality-oriented manner possible.

10. Establish a system of advanced concepts groups (ACG).

    The purpose of these groups is to think outside the box; to push the envelope; to make things lighter, smaller, and stronger; to reduce the number of parts or subsystems; to extend the life cycle; to reduce serviceability; to enhance simplicity and maintainability; and to reduce manufacturing or operating costs. ACGs can also be used to solve customer problems.

11. Do not ...

    - ... allow the drive for greater profits to degrade the quality, performance, or system life of your products.
    - ... permit the drive for greater profits to place unrealistic work requirements on your people or their safety.
    - ... allow the desire to reduce costs to eliminate positions or functions or outsourcing.

    So many times, such "do not" decisions incur greater costs, poor morale, and lack of trust in leadership.

Checklist

- ✓ Have you forgotten why you were chosen to lead the organization?
- ✓ Are there any restrictions to revisit?
- ✓ Are you doing what you set out to accomplish?
- ✓ Are you monitoring all key organizational measures?
- ✓ Have you clearly identified your expectations to your leadership team?
- ✓ Are you fully utilizing all available communication capabilities to keep workforce, customers, suppliers, and superiors informed?
- ✓ Are you accomplishing walkabouts?
- ✓ Are you removing "problem children"?
- ✓ Are you removing or reassigning managers who cannot manage?

> Leadership is a skill, even an art form. It is taught in an educational environment and learned through the experience of being in charge or observing those who are. Very few people are born leaders. Most individuals receive various forms of training, whether through a classroom or on the job. Not all come out being leaders—for whatever reason. Some just do not get it, while others consume everything and grow their leadership skills into something to admire.
>
> Historically, many leaders are born during crises, when they take control and preclude disaster. Unlike any other organization, the Department of Defense spends millions of dollars on leadership and management training to ensure that its officers and noncommissioned officers can lead others in very fluid combat situations and other crises to achieve positive results. Such individuals may know very little, if anything, about the business or the organization, but they *do* understand people, organization dynamics, and how to get the job done.

Being chosen to lead is a great opportunity. We put everything we have learned into play to make the organization more successful. What makes you a better leader is never allowing yourself to think that you know everything. You must expect to make mistakes and learn from them, as well as the mistakes of others. Never be afraid of making decisions based on all available information. You must also be willing to modify or change a bad decision based on new information or a change in the original situation. Making no decision at all is much worse.

Successful leaders are in a constant learning mode, always learning from the best as well as the worst. Never forgetting who you are, where you came from, and the people who got you where you are enables you to put challenges in perspective, thus allowing better decisions and focus. Good leaders always take care of their people, and they, in turn, take care of their leader.

STRATEGY 7

Create a Positive Work Environment

One of a leader's more enjoyable challenges is to create a positive work environment that provides people with a safe, professional work area with unlimited opportunities to grow within their job. Whether it is an office setting, a research lab, a prototype facility or a production floor, many of the challenges are similar but deployed differently. Most people enjoy going to work if they know that their work is valued. By providing as much latitude and flexibility, it appreciably increases the benefits of such a work environment.

Rules

- Provide a positive work environment.
- Provide a secure, safe and professional work environment.
- Provide all the resources necessary for individuals to do their job.
- Celebrate individual, team and organizational achievements.
- Communicate, communicate, and communicate.
- Use organizational measures to indicate progress.

Key Points:

1. Create a safe work environment that encourages individual and team success through innovative thinking, empowerment, and growth.

2. Create an environment that encourages individuals to seek additional training and education to grow individually and professionally.
3. Create an environment that eliminates bottlenecks.
4. Create an environment that promotes the highest level of ethical and professional behavior.
5. Create an environment that prohibits racists, sexist, and unethical behavior.
6. Implement a process that provides multiple opportunities for individuals to discuss their ideas, concerns, opinions, and frustrations.
7. Provide coaching and mentoring as often as possible.
8. Find the right fit.
9. Avoid pitfalls that can undermine the goal of building a strong positive work environment.

Discussion

1. Create a safe work environment that encourages individual and team success through innovative thinking, empowerment, and growth.

    - Provide as much latitude and flexibility as possible to allow individuals and teams to use their creativity and imagination in finding better ways of doing their job. Ensure that all persons understand any established boundaries to their empowerment.

    - If possible, allow teams some latitude in designing their work area.

    - Encourage individuals and teams to offer continuous improvement suggestions regarding any facet of organization's operations, policies or processes.

    - Be sensitive to any environment that could use:

- o better lighting, heating or cooling;
- o larger space allocations, noise reduction, or better paint schemes;
- o more ergonomic furniture or more advanced computers and software; or
- o a break room, eating areas, and multipurpose room.

2. Create an environment that encourages individuals to seek additional training and education to grow individually and professionally.

   - Offer as many job-related programs as possible to help individuals improve their personal and professional core competencies, as well as other job skills.

   - Work with human resources to identify local technical schools and universities that offer courses on campus during and after regular work hours.

   - If possible, identify specific positions that allow cross-training—for example, into a job that's strongly desired, but the individual has little training. This action will appreciably improve morale and pay tremendous dividends during peak workloads.

3. Create an environment that eliminates bottlenecks.

   - One of the first indicators that progress is being made in the effort to improve the work environment is an increase in the identification of bottlenecks or problem areas. A rapid response to solicit a fix or a better process encourages those making the suggestion to think through the purpose and requirements of the process. It reduces finger-pointing and generates ownership and support for any new process.

   - Forward suggestions to customer for eliminating bottlenecks their processes or requirements generate.

4. Create an environment that promotes the highest levels of ethical and professional behavior.

    - Organizational leaders and managers set the tone for professional behavior by following corporate policies and procedures. These individuals have so much influence throughout the company when they model professional, courteous, and straightforward behavior. They can quickly address perceived or actual unacceptable behavior, which provides a backdrop for fostering a high standard of ethics. There is no substitute.

5. Create an environment that prohibits racist, sexist, or unethical behavior.

    - Do not allow unacceptable behavior by anyone, anytime or anywhere.

    - Clearly communicate and openly display policies regarding such behavior throughout the organization in the form of posters, leadership letters, and policy statements. Clearly convey the levels of disciplinary action up to and including dismissal.

    - Investigate any real or perceived behavior quickly. Removing or reassigning individuals may be appropriate until an inquiry is completed and action is taken.

6. Implement a process that provides multiple opportunities for individuals to discuss their ideas, concerns, opinions, and frustrations. Such a process may include the following:

    - an open-door policy that encourages individuals to periodically meet with their managers to discuss ideas, suggestions, and/or complaints

    - a website that individuals can use anonymously to voice their opinions, concerns, recommendations, and frustrations

    - a formal suggestion program that offers financial reward

- an open-season survey for persons to identify functions, policies, and processes that work well, need modification, or need elimination

At the completion of any process, provide feedback to the individual or group as to how valuable their ideas, suggestions and initiatives have been toward making organizational improvements.

7. Provide coaching and mentoring as often as possible.

    - Implement a program that encourages subject-matter experts and other, more experienced teammates to coach or mentor junior individuals. This provides an opportunity for new members to learn how real-world challenges were resolved from a technical, management, or functional point of view. While universities provide an excellent backdrop for science and technology, it is industry that takes it to the next several levels of application, utility and integration—such as designing, building, and testing a stealth platform.

    - If possible, fund working luncheons and internal seminars.

8. Find the right fit.

    For whatever reason, there are times when highly qualified, dedicated, hard-working individuals are not producing the results desired. Rather than allow the situation to continue, it is more beneficial to work with those individuals to find the right fit for their skills and talents. Finding the right fit is so much more rewarding for everyone and sends a very positive message to all personnel.

9. Avoid pitfalls that can undermine the goal of building a strong positive work environment.

    - Nepotism, while a smart strategy for a family-owned business, is not appropriate for a non-family-owned business unless the organization is very large and family members work in different departments and locations, and under different management chains.

- Favoritism violates the basic ground rule that everyone is to be treated the same. Be consistent and use established programs to reward outstanding performance.

- Large pay gaps for the same job, experience level, and education requirements lead to poor morale. Task human resources to review all job offers against a job matrix to preclude such a problem. If a problem is identified, resolve for the lower paid individual receiving an increase. Never allow such gaps based on gender.

- Unrealistic policies leads to disrespect for all rules. Organize a multi-departmental team to review and make recommendations regarding any policy or process identified as unrealistic.

- Disciplinary action for the same offense must not be inconsistent. Set a policy and enforce it.

- Senior level managers hired with little or no real management or leadership experience or track record within the organization and/or industry will have trouble gaining the respect of workers.

- Avoid any appearance or perception of an old boy network—or a feminist brigade.

- Keeping incompetent managers or leadership-team members on the job is unwise and somewhat stupid. Once a manager or leadership team member demonstrates that the job is over his or her head, remove that individual and allow the number-two to assume the duties until a replacement is identified.

- Remove any level of manager who openly criticizes organizational decisions or policies.

- Reverse bad decisions based on bad information or advice. Doing so at once is not as embarrassing as letting the mistake snowball.

Checklist

- ✓ Are policies and processes in place to encourage people to think outside the box?
- ✓ Are policies, processes, and support systems in place to allow people to communicate their ideas, suggestions, opinions, concerns, and frustrations?
- ✓ Are policies regarding unethical, sexist, or racist behavior clearly communicated throughout the organization in written, visual and electronic formats and highlighted during new-employee orientations?
- ✓ Are open-season survey findings and corrective actions communicated to the workforce?
- ✓ Are educational opportunities posted on the organization's website and throughout the company?

Creating a positive work environment while coping with organizational challenges is every leader's continuing goal. Building a strong level of employee satisfaction has so many positive benefits; it reduces absenteeism, turnovers, and discipline situations while encouraging accountability and ownership for personal performance. Other benefits include higher production of quality products and services, greater customer satisfaction, and ultimately increased business.

STRATEGY 8

Communicate

In an age where news is frequently communicated as it happens, employees want to know about any organizational situation that affects them directly or indirectly, whether positive or negative. Timely communication is critical to precluding inaccurate or incomplete data. Use all available media capabilities to ensure speedy information flow throughout the organization.

Rules

- Transmit time-sensitive organizational information promptly to superiors and direct reports.
- Use stand-ups and one-on-ones to provide more detail.
- Make sure all official communications use proper English and are free of grammatical errors.
- Ensure customer contractual transmissions are done in compliance with the requirements of the contract.
- Mark all proprietary and/or classified information in accordance with organizational or customer marking guides.

Key Points

1. Timely information flow is critical to organizational success.
2. Use common sense to keep the boss, direct reports, organization, customers, and suppliers informed of pertinent information.

3. Use stand-ups and routine staff meetings to convey information, direction, focus, and guidance.
4. Use the most effective media products to display the organization's vision, mission, core values, and goals.
5. Connect the dots between teamwork, quality, cost, security, customer satisfaction, continued success, and job security.
6. Develop an internal communications plan that, among other things, identifies six to eight key messages that warrant periodic emphasis during the year.

Discussion

1. Timely information flow is critical to organizational success.

   - Keep people informed regarding the health of the organization and how its successes, challenges, and downturns affect them directly and indirectly. Get the official word out using all available communication media. Any significant delay in getting information disseminated will produce incorrect or erroneous data, speculation, and rumors. It is wiser to communicate updates—even with corrections—than wait for the whole story. It is also imperative that all communications be error-free.

   - Hosting all-hands meetings can be most beneficial. The leadership team can discuss subjects that need attention while giving employees a chance to ask questions and voice concerns and frustrations.

2. Use common sense to keep the boss, direct reports, organization, customers, and suppliers informed of pertinent information.

   - The main goal is to keep each briefed on those issues that are important to them in the fastest manner possible. Using face time, emails, texts (if applicable), verbal communications, messaging, or conference calls should achieve the objective. Timely communications are essential, especially if the information is less than positive.

- Implement a process to identify which data is stored for future reference and compliance. Be sensitive to discussing or transmitting proprietary information on any electronic device. Depending on the organization's business, using encrypted communication software and devices may be wise; government customers may supply such capabilities.

3. Use stand-ups and routine staff meetings to convey information, direction, focus, and guidance.

    - A dynamic organization will require more meetings. The primary purpose is to give, receive, and share information while updating guidance, instructions, and priorities. Use stand-ups, in which the attendees remain standing, to achieve rapid information transfer.

    - It is important to keep such meetings focused and as short as possible. The very purpose of stand-ups is to keep the meeting short, fifteen to thirty minutes. Sit-down staff meetings have a tendency to last thirty to sixty minutes and wander off the subject more frequently. New information, concerns, or feedback may warrant scheduling a topic-specific meeting with the applicable participants. As a minimum, each meeting should cover the following if there is new information for the specific item (note that this is the same fixed agenda as in strategy 6.1):
        o special recognition
        o announcements from higher headquarters
        o emphasis of or changes to organizational policies or processes
        o key personnel assignments
        o current business updates
        o customer announcements or feedback
        o quality issues
        o security and safety issues
        o operational issues (administrative, personnel, finance, facilities)

- current tasking updates
- new tasking
- rumor mill
- any last-minute pop-ups that require attention

4. Use the most effective media products available to display the organization's vision, mission, core values, and goals.

    - Key topics should be clearly visible and communicated using the most appealing words and graphics appropriate to convey the seriousness of each topic. A multimedia display should be exhibited at each organizational facility entrance, on the walls of major conference rooms and auditoriums; it should also be the introductory visual for formal presentations. If permitted or appropriate, incorporate it into formal bids and proposals.

    - Clearly express and discuss each topic during new-employee orientations. Question-and-answer periods will encourage additional dialogue to help convey the meaning and seriousness of each topic.

5. Connect the dots between teamwork, quality, cost, security, customer satisfaction, continued success, and job security.

    - Use the website and various visual media to link success with product quality, price, customer satisfaction, and job security. Use statistical measures whenever possible to show trends.

    - Convey what initiatives are available to improve the quality or capabilities of a product, to extend product warranties, and to reduce production costs.

6. Develop an internal communications plan that, among other things, identifies six to eight key messages that warrant periodic emphasis during the year. Include messages that address the following:

    - organizational ethics and professional conduct
    - teamwork and respect

- product quality
- customer satisfaction
- continuous improvement
- team-member empowerment
- pushing the envelope
- opportunities to excel

Checklist

✓ Are routine meetings scheduled with their purpose and guidelines defined? Do they use a fixed agenda?
✓ Are processes in place to communicate information to all relevant parties in a prompt manner?
✓ Is there a communications plan that identifies key messages?
✓ Are the key messages being communicated?
✓ Are the organization's vision, mission, core values, and goals on display throughout the company and included in new employee orientation?
✓ Is communication effectiveness included in the annual open-season survey?

We live in a world where news and events are frequently transmitted as they happen. People want to know what is happening within their organization. Therefore, it is important to use all available electronic and visual media to spread the word in addition to staff meetings and stand-ups. I have heard people say that stand-ups and staff meetings are a waste of time. Frequently, these very same people complain that they are not getting information in a timely manner. Such meetings are vital in high-octane organizations where budgets, schedules, and expectations are closely monitored. Frequency and length of routine meetings are dictated by the type of business.

STRATEGY 9

Take Care of the Boss

Your boss is the most important person in your reporting chain. Take the initiative to understand this individual on multiple levels. It is important that you know his or her expectations and hot buttons. There is no limit to the upside of building a good relationship. This individual can make your life challenging, rewarding, and enjoyable. Conversely, this same person can make your life extremely stressful.

For those individuals who have a functional and a program boss, the same applies to both. Each can open opportunity doors you did not know existed.

Rules

- Your most important job is your current job.
- Take the initiative to get to know your boss.
- Keep shared confidences to yourself.
- Always keep the boss informed to preclude blindsiding.
- Complete the boss's tasks on or before their due date.
- Never give your boss a poorly written, incomplete report.
- Never embarrass your boss in a negative manner.
- Learn your boss's written and unwritten policies.
- Never intentionally mislead or deceive your boss.
- Never criticize your boss to your team, your peers, or boss's superiors.

Key Points

1. Your boss is the most important person in your organizational chain.
2. Employ a proactive communication approach with the boss.
3. Be sensitive to and comply with your boss's written and unwritten policies.
4. Give top priority to your boss's tasks.
5. When appropriate, invite the boss to participate in recognition events.
6. Initiate "How goes it?" discussions.
7. Manage multiple bosses.
8. Know when it is time to leave.

Discussion

1. Your boss is the most important person in your organizational chain.

    It is very prudent that you get to know your boss on as many levels as possible—professional, social, academic, sports, etc. Your boss has the power to make your job challenging, exciting, and rewarding. He or she can give you greater responsibility, visibility, and authority, and open new upward opportunities for you. Bosses can highlight your successes or failures to their superiors in whatever light they wish to either grow or limit your career. A good boss will always highlight the accomplishments and talents of his or her people while mentioning improvement areas in private.

2. Employ a proactive communication approach with the boss.
    - Use one-on-ones to get to know your boss, learn expectations, pass on information, and understand priorities and unwritten policies. Nothing could be worse than your boss finding out about a problem, issue, or challenge that directly affects the department from someone other than you.

- Extend communication in the following ways:
  - Ask your boss to clarify any restrictions or limitations to your authority.
  - Use emails or texts to keep the boss informed on any time-sensitive issues.
  - Provide a weekly activities report (WAR) to keep your boss informed while providing good documentation for everyone concerned. The WAR should be short and only cover those items important to the boss.
  - Observe and participate in scheduled staff meetings, stand-ups, program reviews, and other business meetings.
  - If appropriate, social events offer opportunities to discuss ideas and suggestions.

  Each of the approaches above will help you determine if this individual is the type who will provide a lot of management oversight or very little. The sooner you find out, the more effectively you can perform your job. Until trust is established, it is common for new bosses to have additional oversight or interject themselves into your operations. If it becomes a problem, advise the boss that you need more latitude to do your job.

- At meetings that involve senior organizational leaders, if questioned, it is often prudent to say that you will get the answer for them rather than giving an unresearched or negative reply. As other agendas may be in play, it would be wiser to discuss more in-depth answers or perceptions with your boss before responding.

3. Be sensitive to and comply with your boss's written and unwritten policies.

    These policies could vary from working schedules to dress codes, to office music, to office decorations, to working relationships, to customer contacts, to travel guidelines, to overtime compensation. The point is to be aware of these policies and comply with them.

4. Give top priority to your boss's tasks.

   Whenever you receive a verbal or written task from the boss, do not assume details. Ask for any clarification, confirm the due date if not given, and immediately start to work. Notify the boss of any issue that might influence your ability to complete the task and your approach to work around the issue.

5. When appropriate, invite the boss to participate in recognition events.

   Most bosses love to participate in award events. However, having a senior alternate stand-in may be prudent. Provide time in the schedule for the boss to address any hot topics or answer questions, if he or she is agreeable.

6. Initiate "How goes it?" discussions.

   If you ever sense a potential problem between you and your boss, simply ask. Your immediate goal is to get your boss to talk to you—the sooner, the better. There are many reasons that a problem might exist. Whatever the reason, it is always advisable to be proactive in these situations.

7. Manage multiple bosses.

   It is common in today's work environment to have a functional and a program boss, especially in large organizations. If you were hired to provide full-time support to a specific program, project, or initiative, you will likely have a program boss as well as a functional boss who provides more administrative support to you. The functional boss will also be your performance evaluator with inputs from your program boss. Therefore, it is important to keep both in the information loop.

8. Know when it is time to leave
   - Bad bosses can come in many forms. They can be arrogant and self-serving; incompetent minimalists; or indecisive and finger-pointing toads. They can also be unethical, lying, and cheating climbers who are jealous of anyone who receives positive recognition. Whatever form they come in, if you know someone who has these qualities, you must always be professional, courteous and respectful. Above all, keep your opinions to yourself. Some guidelines:
     - Keep copies of correspondence, emails, and texts, both favorable and unfavorable.
     - Keep documentation of any verbal and written tasks.
     - Keep bosses informed of all tasks status and keep records of any significant situation that could affect the task.
   - We can all live and work for people who have their share of flaws. When their problems start affecting our work and private lives, it is time to look elsewhere.
   - Some indications that it is time to look for another job include the following:
     - Tasks that normally go to you are given to someone else.
     - The flow of information from management stops.
     - When approached, the boss passes you off.
     - Other individuals are given credit for work you did.
     - You get lower marks on performance reviews, lower pay raises, and low or no bonuses.
   - If you prefer to remain in the organization, ask your boss to recommend you for another position outside that individual's area. If that is not doable, meet with human resources to look for positions elsewhere, or ask a superior for help finding a different job elsewhere.

Checklist

- ✓ What is your boss's vision?
- ✓ What are your boss's goals and objectives?
- ✓ What are your boss's performance expectations and measures?
- ✓ What are your boss's hot buttons?
- ✓ What are your boss's unwritten policies?
- ✓ Has your boss answered all questions regarding his or her position?
- ✓ Has your boss identified any restrictions or limitations?
- ✓ Has your boss identified a staff or other meeting schedule?
- ✓ Has your boss identified a preferred method of communication?
- ✓ Has an after-duty communication method been identified?

As previously stated, I have worked for and with some of the finest and most professional, dedicated, intelligent, and mission-oriented leaders one could find. These persons constantly set the performance bar high to challenge the individual and collective creative energies of their people. It was very easy to go the extra mile, to stay late, and to work on weekends for such individuals. What I learned from them was invaluable in terms of maintaining good communications, measuring performance, promoting a sense of excellence, and being a good leader and manager.

STRATEGY 10

Picking New Leadership-Team Members Wisely

When you interview for a leadership position, ask if you can pick a new leadership team, move members around, and fill new or vacant positions. Another possible action is to reassign underperforming members or those individuals whose allegiance to the outgoing leadership is interfering with their performance. The best of all worlds is to select and build a leadership team from scratch; thus, all teammates are on the same page from the start.

The organization's success depends on everyone working together. When one company buys another, it frequently replaces the entire leadership team. Such a move, coupled with new processes and procedures, expedites the transition of culture. Otherwise, a great deal of intellectual and emotional energy is wasted.

Rules

Leadership team in place

- Request a résumé or biography from each team member.
- Meet frequently with members individually and collectively on and off campus.
- Build a relationship with each member on as many levels as possible.

- Invite their participation in selecting new members.
- Remove "problem children" from the leadership ranks.

Building a new leadership team

- Seek nominees from those who selected you.
- Advance high-performing individuals who have proven their leadership and management skills within the organization.
- Publish vacancy announcements throughout the organization.
- Use all applicable professional networks to identify other candidates.
- Have an extensive background check completed on each applicant.

Key Points

1. Build a close working relationship with each leadership-team member.
2. Get members involved in nominating and down-selecting new members.
3. Have human resources (HR) post vacancy announcements on the organization's website for at least two weeks.
4. Have HR develop a separate list of qualified candidates based on their leadership, management, communication, organizational, and overall people skills, as noted in annual performance reviews.
5. Be willing to reassign those leadership-team members who do not demonstrate the skills needed to lead and manage their organization.
6. Remove immediately anyone in a leadership position who openly or publicly exhibits racist, sexist, discriminatory, or unethical behavior until an inquiry is completed.
7. Be willing to dismiss any leadership-team member who publicly criticizes the goals, plans, decisions, and approach of the leadership team or individual team members.
8. Evaluate the short list of applicants.

Discussion

1. Build a close working relationship with each leadership-team member.

    - Meet with your team members individually and collectively on and off campus to get to know them and enhance communications between them. Hosting off-site meetings can produce excellent results. It allows members to relax while getting to know each other on a professional and social bases. Establishing goals and ground rules for the meeting will keep it focused. Goals may include identifying new initiatives to improve product quality, reduce overhead costs, or expand the business base. Ground rules may include leaving cell phones at the door while keeping all discussions positive, honest, and straightforward. Encouraging senior members to discuss their career and the lessons learned can benefit everyone.

    - Scheduling each member to present an organizations and functions (O&F) presentation to include current challenges, programs, new initiatives, and customer feedback will benefit everyone, especially new members.

2. Get members involved in nominating and down-selecting new members.

    Always solicit current team members for their recommendations for new and projected vacancies. Ask them to interview the short-list candidates.

3. Have human resources (HR) post vacancy announcements on the organization website for at least two weeks.

    Posting is a smart way to identify individuals overlooked by the system. It also sends a very positive message to those wishing to advance, take on more responsibility, or see a long-term career with the organization.

4. Have HR develop a separate list of qualified candidates based on their leadership, management, communication, organizational, and overall people skills, as noted in annual performance reviews.

   Ask HR to look for individuals with a proven performance record for leading and managing multi-disciplined, diverse teams.

5. Be willing to reassign those leadership-team members who do not demonstrate the skills needed to lead and manage their organization.

   Every function within an organization has various measures to show performance—or lack thereof. Use trend lines, historical data, and customer or supplier inputs to make such a decision. Normally, nonperformers already have a negative reputation and "people problems," as indicated by complaints, grievances, transfers, and possible lawsuits.

6. Remove immediately anyone in a leadership position who openly or publicly demonstrates racist, sexist, discriminatory, or unethical behavior until an inquiry is completed.

   This is unacceptable behavior for anyone, much less a leadership-team member. It is important to "walk the talk" until an inquiry is completed and the charges are found to be inaccurate or untrue.

7. Be willing to dismiss any leadership-team member who publicly criticizes the goals, plans, decisions, and approach of the leadership team or individual team members.

   A leadership team's success depends on the willingness and ability of each team member to work with and support the other, even if they do not totally agree. Leadership-team meetings are the place for open, frank discussions that consider all opinions and data points before reaching a consensus and making a decision. To agree to disagree is expected and encouraged; however, to take a critical issue public is entirely another matter and is unacceptable. This also applies to senior management personnel.

8. Evaluate the short list of applicants.

    - Using HR guidelines, ask current members to interview each candidate on the short list in multiple settings on and off campus with a final evaluation and recommendation.

    - While all candidates should be subject matter experts (SMEs) in their given profession, they should also exhibit the following:
        o personality and interpersonal skills to successfully lead, direct, nurture, and mentor their team members
        o the ability to develop teams that fully understand their role in making the organization successful by working with and supporting the work of other groups
        o an absence of confrontational, finger-pointing, racist, sexist, or narcissistic behavior
        o an openness to change and continuous improvement
        o a desire for excellence, quality products, and customer service
        o a willingness to delegate responsibility and accountability
        o comfort with being a coach, champion, and cheerleader

Checklists

✓ Have all leadership-team bios been collected and reviewed?
✓ Do backgrounds support the current job?
✓ Does each position have a current description?
✓ Have off-site meetings been scheduled, goals identified, and ground rules established?
✓ Have O&F presentations been scheduled?
✓ Are processes in place to select new team members?
✓ Are processes in place for removing team members for unacceptable behavior?

Too frequently, I have seen individuals selected for key positions without the experience or proven record needed as a leader or manager. The consequence of such selections was typically an increase in leadership and management issues that reflected poorly on them. Several individuals were reassigned while a few were let go. It is critical to take whatever time necessary to pick the right people for a leadership team, as each team member is crucial in making the organization successful. Building a cohesive team that uses a consensus decision-making process will produce better decisions, strategies, and overall direction for the organization. While this method encourages each member to provide greater input, there are some decisions that only you, the organizational leader, can make. Team members who cannot comply with the decisions of the team or publically criticize team member decisions, strategies, or plans should be immediately reassigned or fired.

STRATEGY 11

Taking Care of the People and the Organization

The truest measure of success for a leader is the ability to transform the organization into an industrial leader for quality products, service, work environment, and profitability. Positioning the company for stability and competitiveness is what we do as leaders and senior managers—it is the purpose of leadership. Leaving an organization that we have devoted our whole self to, for whatever reason, can be extremely tough; but to leave it as a true winner is the most precious gift we can extend to the friends and colleagues we leave behind.

> The following is a short composite of various key principles discussed throughout the book that warrant additional emphasis. They are essential to the continued success of any organization.

Rules

- Pick leadership-team members who value their people, product quality, and first-class customer satisfaction.
- People are an organization's most valued asset.
- Offer personal and professional growth opportunities.

- Build a culture that encourages individuals to seek better ways to design, produce, sell, and service high-quality products that exceed customer expectations.
- Share business successes with all personnel to build a more dedicated and loyal workforce.

Key Points

1. People create success.
2. Choose proven people-oriented people for the leadership team.
3. Offer personal and professional growth opportunities.
4. Build a culture that demands high standards.
5. Maintain a safe work environment.
6. Keep the workforce informed.
7. Maintain an internal feedback system.
8. Maintain budget discipline for overhead and program costs.
9. Maintain a profit-sharing program based on annual performance.

Discussion

1. People create success.

    It is people who do everything that makes the organization function. They improve it, fix it, and grow it. They create new products and services, improve current operations, and fix the things that break. It is people who keep products and services evolving and customers happy.

2. Choose proven people-oriented people for the leadership team.

    Take time to find individuals who demonstrate a true concern for their people to lead and manage larger teams within the organization. Unless there is a reason not to, always look inside the organization first. Posting a position and having other leadership-team members conduct the first, second, and possibly the third interview may be appropriate to best identify a candidate's strengths, limitations, and priorities. While it is important that candidates be experts in their field, proven leadership and management skills are more critical for team-leadership positions.

3. Offer personal and professional growth opportunities.

    - Most workers want a chance to grow within their job, chosen profession, and level of responsibility. They want to believe that the prospect of upward mobility exists and is attainable if they possess the basic job qualifications (for example, degree, license, or certification). A flexible manning process allows and encourages individuals to compete for other positions, which will not only satisfy their personal goals but also do wonders for workforce stability.

    - It is a smart move for organizations to allow high-performing managers to supervise any department or profession and keep the team focused, on track, within budget, and on schedule.

    - Nontechnical managers can successfully manage a highly technical team if a strong technical person fills the number-two position. This pairing will help to eliminate various interpretation problems; of course, there are always exceptions in our specialized world. It is okay—and a frequent occurrence—for managers to make less than the people they manage.

4. Build a culture that demands high standards.

    - Create an organizational culture that embraces a positive and continuous improvement mind-set, respect for fellow workers, and a strong sense of ethics. These qualities will serve as the foundation for building and enhancing teamwork. Establishing a work environment that channels individual and team energies to seek better ways of building higher-quality products will produce tangible measurable results. Encouraging and challenging individuals and teams to think outside the box will tap an impressive amount of collective thinking that could achieve results not yet attainable.

- One of the most important and rewarding things a leader can do for an organization is to implement and maintain policies that nurture such a work environment. Numerous studies report that happy, challenged individuals perform their functions better, while giving more back to the organization in terms of time, energy, and intellectual contribution. Specifically, these individuals take pride in and ownership of the team's success and reputation; go the extra mile in performing their work; readily support each other and other teams; and are willing to complete tasks outside their function.

5. Maintain a safe work environment.

Nobody wants to work in an unsafe work environment that may be falling apart, with equipment that sparks, a high level of noise, poor ventilation, and few exits. Thanks to numerous laws, such workspaces should be closed down. Report and correct immediately any real or perceived work hazard without exception. Safety is paramount for any organization. Encourage individuals to report any situation that could put anyone in danger.

6. Keep the workforce informed.

We live in an information age and have intelligent individuals working for us who want to be kept informed. Expeditiously communicate positive and negative information to preclude rumors. If applicable, inform workers that more details will be provided as they become available.

7. Maintain an internal feedback system.

Whether we call it an open-door policy or ask employees to complete an annual open-season survey, we need to maintain a system that allows individuals to vent their unfiltered frustrations and suggestions. Often such input identifies areas for review and improvement.

8. Maintain budget discipline for overhead and program costs.

   Do not allow budget overages for operating the organization or managing a direct-charge program without a short term get-well date; otherwise, it is a recipe for disaster. Keep an overhead and program-measurement system that identifies potential problems as far in advance as possible. Be willing to reassign any manager who has a history of not being able to maintain fiscal discipline.

9. Maintain a profit-sharing program based on annual performance.

   This incentive program is one of the most powerful ways of rewarding people for their work, dedication, and reliability. It builds loyalty and ownership for organizational success. Distribute quarterly measures to the workforce in a timely manner.

Checklist

- ✓ Is the right leadership team in place?
- ✓ Is there an annual review of work environment policies and processes?
- ✓ Are individuals being encouraged to take advantage of training opportunities?
- ✓ Are individuals being encouraged to apply for vacant management positions?
- ✓ Are safety concerns reported and corrected in a timely manner?
- ✓ Have expectations for leading, managing, and building a positive work environment been clearly communicated and documented on performance appraisals?
- ✓ Do management assessments include multiple leadership and management measures to capture an individual's actual performance and potential?
- ✓ Are profit-sharing communications current?

To ensure continued organizational success long after we have departed, the most lasting gift we can give the organization is a leadership team capable of taking it to the next level of success. Taking time to pick the right people to lead and manage various levels within the organization will produce tremendous dividends. Creating an environment that nurtures continuous improvement and gets everyone thinking outside the box will reduce costs, improve quality, expand the customer base, and increase sales. Incorporating process-management techniques will control overhead and program costs by reducing non-value-added work. By integrating these techniques, we can turn a good organization into a world-class organization that can flourish during upturns and survive downturns. This process will protect the people and ensure that the organization is operating long after we have gone.

STRATEGY 12

Staff for a Stable Labor Force

A challenge for any organization is to keep a stable labor force with the right combination of skill sets and skill mixes, experience, and proficiency through economic upturns and downturns. A strategy that facilitates a stable, loyal workforce, a large part-time labor pool, and a competitive compensation package helps to reduce the challenge.

Rules

- Identify projected staffing requirements.
- Seek smart, well-qualified individuals with a positive attitude.
- Continually expand the part-time labor pool.
- Never retain employees who lied about their background to get hired.

Key Points

1. Maintain an experienced human resources (HR) team.
2. Raise awareness.
3. Implement an 80/20 staffing rule.
4. Build a large labor pool to accommodate workload spikes.
5. Establish a "fully employed" rule.
6. Perform walkabouts.

7. Do not keep new personnel who lied about their experience, degrees, certifications, or citizenship.
8. Release individuals who lie, cheat, or steal.
9. Watch for indicators of overstaffing or an unbalanced skill mix.

Discussion

1. Maintain an experienced human resources (HR) team.

    - Any sizable organization requires a professional HR leader and team to support current and projected staffing requirements while ensuring compliance with all state and federal guidelines. The need exists for a very proactive team that thinks outside the box when it comes to recruitment, planning, protecting individual rights, and conducting programs that help people grow in their job.

    - At a minimum, a HR program needs to do the following:

        o Identify skill sets and skill mixes that meet current and projected organizational requirements.

        o Identify the best sources for each skill requirement.

        o Field a recruitment process to find highly qualified candidates (civilians, veterans and college graduates) who demonstrate a positive attitude.

        o Retain an application that also functions as a contract for ethical behavior, professional conduct, and a non-disclosure agreement (NDA) to protect proprietary and customer information. This application should hold up in a court of law and allow the organization to run a credit report.

        o Collect copies of a candidate's birth certificate or passport, degrees, certifications, licenses, DD form 214, pay slips, and any other information required by the organization or its customers.

o   Keep a position description (PD) for each full-time, part-time, and contractor position to delineate its functions and responsibilities.

o   Coordinate an interview process to select senior professionals that may include multiple interviews with various teams and subject-matter experts (SMEs). Questions should evaluate experience levels, attitude, requirements of the job, and appropriateness to the organization's mission. The team's task is to validate the candidate's credentials, level of experience, competence, skill level, attitude, and desire to join the organization.

o   Conduct initial and follow-up orientation classes that include, but are not limited to, safety, security, leave policies, work schedules, education, diversity, drug and alcohol abuse, sexual harassment, unacceptable body contact, racial bigotry or jokes, and unacceptable behaviors that could result in the individual's release.

o   Assign a sponsor for each new full-time employee.

o   Initiate an annual performance review for each employee. At a minimum, it should measure individual job performance, communications skills, team support, compliance, attention to detail, and ethical behavior. If applicable, it should also address the individual's leadership and management skills, and quality and customer-support orientation.

o   Recruits hired to support a government contract may have a delayed reporting date because of the government vetting process that starts soon after signing the offer letter. Additional forms may be required for positions that require a security clearance. Advise those individuals considered for classified positions in writing that any job offer is contingent on satisfying all customer security clearance requirements within the given timeframe; if not, the offer could become void.

- If applicable, HR policies that should be reviewed annually by the leadership team include the following:
    o part-time position identification and allocation
    o hiring, firing, and harassment policies
    o hiring family members
    o probation period lengths
    o celebrating birthdays, anniversaries, or childbirths
    o special out-of-cycle monetary awards
- Many large corporations have the flexibility to allow couples to work within the company as long as they work in different management chains or geographical locations. However, it is ill-advised to allow husbands, wives, significant others, or companions to work within the same organization and the same management chain. Should two individuals marry or decide to cohabitate, place these individuals in different management chains and geographical locations as soon as practical.

2. Raise awareness.

The leadership team should periodically review staffing projections against high-value contracts, new phases, potential cancellations, and closeouts. Program managers should identify changes in their contracts as far into the future as possible.

3. Implement an 80/20 staffing rule.

- Significant ups and downs in business, contracts, sales, workload, funding, and profits are a given. One approach to reducing the impact on staffing is to implement the 80/20 rule or one that functions in a similar way. The organization identifies 80 percent of its staffing requirements as full-time positions and the remaining 20 percent as part-time/temporary/independent contractor positions. Many retail businesses have a ratio that is closer to the opposite, or 20/80. Although the numbers vary with the industry, the approach gives the organization greater flexibility in dealing with seasonal swings or substantial business turns.

- Full-time employees have various benefit levels, while temporary persons usually receive a straight hourly or weekly rate of pay. Keeping a higher rate of pay than that of the local area average will attract qualified people who do not want a full-time position or need benefits.

- Acquire temporary personnel from the labor pool or a third party to work less than thirty-two hours per week. Hire independent contractors directly or through a third party to work forty hours per week. Typically, anyone who falls within the 20 percent is the first to go or to have hours decreased during downturns and increased during upturns. It is important that both full-time and temporary personnel know this policy, as it reduces stress for everyone.

- The nature of the organization's core business dictates which elements within the company have full-time or part-time positions. In many firms, more part-time jobs appear in the "support" functions, such as administration, maintenance, security guards, purchasing, HR, finance, and training. Exposure to proprietary or customer-sensitive information should prohibit part-time employee involvement.

- In smaller companies, it is beneficial to identify backup personnel, especially for one-deep positions. A small group of floaters to serve as backups can preclude disruptions in daily operations.

- Modify staffing percentages whenever business projections increase, decrease, or change due to new or lost opportunities.

- The benefits of maintaining a split labor force include the following:
    o Provide a buffer to protect full-time personnel during major downturns or rapid build-ups to meet new obligations.
    o Help management evaluate temporary personnel for full-time positions.

- Let SMEs come onboard for special projects that require unique levels of knowledge and expertise for specific periods.
- Employ talented individuals who do not want a full-time job, such as stay-at-home mothers, retirees, college and trade school students, and even individuals who have full-time jobs: teachers, professors, law enforcement officials, and military members.
- Reduce overall personnel costs.

4. Build a large labor pool to accommodate workload spikes.

Use various recruiting announcements in local newspapers, college bulletin boards, or business and veteran websites to increase the labor pool. Applications should clearly outline the opportunities, guidelines, compensation schedule, any benefits, and an NDA to protect organizational information.

5. Establish a "fully employed" rule.

- When business is booming, management tends to hire any number of folks to do tasks or functions that have never had someone assigned to do them. This practice has a real downside when times get bumpy, as it is difficult to let these folks go, no matter what they do. In this regard, the 80/20 rule benefits everyone, as people understand their situation better.
- A goal of a successful business is to create an environment where team members consider it part of their job to help others inundated with work or are willing to do functions that need doing. Realistically, this does not mean that administrative people can do engineering or technical work, but it does mean that engineers and technical team members can perform administrative, IT, maintenance, and security tasks. A positive byproduct of such involvement is that it results in process improvements that enhance effectiveness,

performance, or productivity while reducing non-value added costs.

- In many organizations, it is nearly impossible to maintain an even workload all the time; however, it is possible to move people between functions to reduce overall costs, maintain a competitive edge, and keep personnel employed.

- Doing more with less and creating an environment of "positive stress" can produce excellent results, as it creates a sense of participation and buy-in by the workforce for organizational performance and success. More important, it reduces nonproductive work hours and rumor-mill time.

- Management should always be sensitive to and watch for possible burnout, which can happen to anyone who works long hours for an extended period. High-performing, dedicated team members frequently overextend themselves to the point that it adversely affects their mental and physical well-being. Burnout can generate more chances for accidents, production problems, quality issues, and safety risks. Intervene immediately whenever there are indications of potential burnout and give such individuals some compensated downtime.

6. Perform walkabouts.

Walkabouts are one of the most effective ways to find out what is going on within the organization. Walking the floors, talking to employees, and viewing work environments, safety measures, and personnel interactions is extremely helpful in gauging the company's posture. These strolls provide another outlook into whether team members appear happy, overworked, or underemployed.

7. Do not keep new personnel who lied about their experience, degrees, certifications, or citizenship.

As soon as it known that an employee lied on his or her résumé or application regarding experience, educations levels, certifications, or previous salaries, dismiss that individual immediately, unless there are extenuating circumstances. Although initial background screening and interviews should uncover such discrepancies, it may be after the employee is hired that such discrepancies are discovered. During the past few decades, in a more competitive job market, an increasing number of people embellish and lie about their education levels, experience, certification, and salary history.

8. Release individuals who lie, cheat or steal.

    Release any employee who lies, cheats, or steals immediately. This includes falsifying documents, time cards, invoices, and travel forms. Clearly communicate other unacceptable behavior during employment orientation and post it throughout the organization. HR, security, and legal should investigate allegations of such behavior immediately if the situation warrants same.

9. Watch for indicators of overstaffing or an unbalanced skill mix, including the following:

    - Too many individuals are walking the halls.
    - People take extended lunch hours and other breaks.
    - People depart before quitting time.
    - Rumors involving customer feedback, internal reassignments, and other issues are increasing.
    - Complaints are increasing regarding minor facility problems, computer glitches, etc.

Checklist

✓ Does the HR team have the necessary resources to accomplish its goals?
✓ Are HR processes current, published, and visually prominent?
✓ Are job vacancies posted on applicable civilian, military, and college websites?

✓ Is the organization in full compliance with state and federal guidelines or have waivers been granted?
✓ Are lessons learned from any HR-related issue being discussed by the leadership team?

> Like any other department or function, HR requires a professional, proactive team with the right skill set and experience level to support organizational staffing goals while ensuring compliance with all applicable state and federal guidelines.
>
> I was fortunate to work with some extremely knowledgeable HR professionals in government and industry. Their knowledge of regulations, labor laws, and direct and indirect charging guidelines made my life much easier. Conversely, I have seen organizations with part-time or inexperienced individuals assigned to do HR tasks. Such organizations have a multitude of personnel problems, which translate into frequent turnover, poor quality, and a lack of emphasis on customer satisfaction.

STRATEGY 13

Hire the Veteran

Military veterans are a tremendous national resource. Our service veterans represent an exceptional, stress-tested resource with numerous skill sets that allow fast assimilation into most organizational structures and cultures. The veteran is a highly trained, disciplined asset who can perform numerous jobs requiring leadership, management, and team-building knowledge with minimum training.

Rules

- Always seek the most qualified individual for each vacant position.
- Never allow a vacancy to impact current or projected business.
- Consider all veterans, including our Wounded Warriors, for organizational vacancies.

Key Points

1. Veterans offer experience levels and skill sets that nonmilitary personnel may not acquire for several years.
2. A veteran's training and level of responsibility frequently far exceed those of their nonmilitary counterparts.
3. Veterans are trained to improvise, remain calm, and think outside the box.
4. Veterans fully understand and appreciate real-world challenges.

Discussion

1. Veterans offer experience levels and skill sets that nonmilitary personnel may not acquire for several years.

   The more senior the veteran, the more experience and skill they have in terms of technical expertise, management, leadership, planning, decision-making, logistics, resource allocation, organization dynamics, communications, administration, security, and team building. Very few civilian counterparts with the same years of experience for the same type of job can compare to the veteran.

2. A veteran's training and level of responsibility frequently far exceed those of their nonmilitary counterparts.

   During their first assignment, veterans complete various levels of formal and hands-on training. They receive corresponding measures of responsibility. Upon each promotion, the veteran is routinely assigned to a position with greater responsibility for managing more resources. Concurrently, the individual typically receives additional leadership and management training, which involves hundreds of hours. Staff jobs expose the veteran to organizational big-picture information, organizational assessments, decision-making, planning, budgeting, and performance measures.

3. Veterans are trained to improvise, remain calm, and think outside the box.

   From their first assignment to the last, veterans accomplish their job and their mission in accordance with established norms. They are taught to remain calm and to think outside the box if norms cannot be followed or resources are not available. Working as individuals and as teams, veterans maximize the utility of all available resources to accomplish their job and their mission. Saving a life, operating a multimillion-dollar piece of equipment, programming IT countermeasures, assessing foreign capabilities, or managing a high-dollar program is simply their day job.

4. Veterans fully understand and appreciate real-world challenges.

   From day one, the veteran is taught to operate in the real world as an individual and a team member. Depending on the situation and the mission, the veteran must be flexible, adaptable, and creative in eliminating pop-up challenges and achieve success, often against overwhelming odds. Veterans fully understand and appreciate the human requirements necessary to be successful in a fast-paced, ever-changing environment.

Checklists

- ✓ Does the organization have a process for recruiting military veterans?
- ✓ Are veteran websites current and used to announce vacancies?
- ✓ Are vacancy announcements and résumé scanners using keywords with military nomenclature or job codes to spot qualified veterans?
- ✓ Has the organization established a goal for hiring veterans?

Having worked in both government and industry, I know that there is little that compares to the amount of leadership, management, and technical training that a veteran receives as compared to industry. While industry's primary practice is to hire an individual with the experience and academic credentials they need, little emphasis is placed on growing personnel to acquire the additional skill sets needed to manage a major activity. When industry program managers are successful in a small program, they are frequently assigned to a much larger one. Should they perform poorly, they are likely reassigned to a lesser role or program.

Although industry frequently pays for and encourages individuals to pursue formal degree programs after work, companies seldom offer academic or professional programs during work hours. Unlike their civilian counterparts, a veteran has hundreds if not thousands of hours of training that add value and technical knowhow to any organization. Part of veterans' job is to receive whatever training is necessary to become efficient, effective, and the best they can be in their chosen career.

There are thousands of highly qualified veterans looking for an opportunity to add value to any organization. Whether the veteran is a stealth engineer, a law-enforcement officer, a program manager, a logistics specialist, a doctor, a planner, an intelligence analyst, a medical technician, an IT specialist, an instructor, or an office manager, each brings a boundless amount of experience, skill, and discipline to the civilian community.

STRATEGY 14

Control Compensation

Controlling labor costs is a critical step in maintaining a competitive overhead rate. Some organizations, to be more competitive domestically and internationally, are lowering executive salaries while offering a bonus or incentive compensation (IC) system tied to overall annual performance. Sizeable direct and indirect labor costs have a negative impact on the organization's ability to keep its products and services competitively priced. Conversely, a compensation strategy that controls labor costs and connects the dots between performance and individual compensation will build a more productive organization and stable workforce.

Strategy 14 only focuses on pay schedules. It does not get into stock purchase plans, stock options, organization-matching plans, 401K plans, or other benefits, such as medical, vacation, or sick leave.

Rules

- Base compensation offers on the requirements, responsibilities, and location of the job.
- Keep compensation in the mid-range, with an annual bonus tied to the organization's performance.
- Compensate both sexes equally for the same job.

- Never pay a new employee higher wages than someone currently doing the same type or level of job.
- Unless there is a reason to do so, do not compensate salaried personnel for hours beyond an average forty-five to fifty hours a week.

Key Points

1. Implement a flexible compensation strategy that offers a competitive wage and annual bonus tied to the organization's performance.
2. Use city, state, and federal labor-rate databases to develop and or compare organizational compensation pay-band schedules.
3. Implement an annual pay-raise policy that includes a percentage tied to inflation and a percentage tied to the individual's overall annual performance.
4. Establish a compensation schedule that pays both sexes the same rate for the same job with the same education and experience levels.
5. Keep the number of executives and senior management positions to a minimum.
6. Establish a system that rewards individual and team results.
7. Consider implementing an attendance program.
8. Be sensitive to the bean counters' primary approach to reducing costs: a reduction in the workforce.

Discussion

1. Implement a flexible compensation strategy that offers a competitive wage and annual bonus tied to the organization's performance.

    Such a strategy will maintain a competitive wage and bonus system that rewards individual performance based on the overall annual performance of the organization. The strategy will help keep labor costs down and organizational rates more viable. Controlling labor costs is a key factor in keeping product and service costs more competitive within the domestic and international markets. The downside of uncontrolled labor costs is layoffs during economic downturns, which encourages individuals to jump ship when the economy improves—thereby making the situation worse.

2. Use city, state, and federal labor-rate databases to develop and/or compare organizational compensation pay-band schedules.

    The HR team has access to various government databases that provide the compensation range for every job one can imagine. The goal is to use this information to establish pay bands based on the mid-range for each job code or category. If necessary, a supplementary location pay may be offered to offset high cost of living in certain areas.

3. Implement an annual pay-raise policy that includes a percentage tied to inflation and a percentage tied to the individual's overall annual performance.

    The inflation percentage should be the same for everyone, while the performance percentage can vary based on an individual's overall annual performance review and justified based on specific accomplishments.

4. Establish a compensation schedule that pays both sexes the same rate for the same job with the same education and experience levels.

    Pay schedules for the same job requiring the same level of education and experience should always be the rule. Accomplish corrections as soon as situations are identified and validated, with the lower-paid individual being given the same compensation as the higher-paid person. Government service is appreciably ahead of industry regarding same pay for same grade and years of service.

5. Keep the number of executives and senior management positions to a minimum.

   As organizations grow, there is a tendency to create new executive-level positions by splitting existing organizations or just creating new titles. Adding new levels of management is ill-advised and frequently equates to a waste of money. Keep the number of executives and senior management positions to the lowest number possible: president, vice president, director, manager, supervisor, and team leader. The workforce easily understands this tight command line. Although some organizations have multiple management levels within each grade, the pecking order can become convoluted and lead to a breakdown of respect for authority.

6. Establish a system that rewards individual and team results.

   Implement a quarterly monetary rewards program to recognize individuals and teams for specific achievements that might include those that increase business, improve a product, reduce costs, or other notable accomplishment.

7. Consider implementing an attendance program.

   I have seen such a program in a major aircraft-manufacturing facility involving thousands of individuals. Statistics show that absenteeism declined appreciably over several years. The program allows individuals to select awards based on the number of years of perfect attendance. More years equal much larger prizes based on the individual's employment anniversary date. The program used gift certificates, gifts, and drawing entries for things like cruises and paid vacations. As long as an individual reports to work and then goes home for whatever reason, it counts as a workday and not a sick or missed day.

8. Be sensitive to the bean counters' primary approach to reducing costs: a reduction in the workforce.

- A common bean-counter (or fiscal) approach to reducing costs is to cut the labor force. There are times when this is the only option to keep the organization operating, but it should be the very last option. Evaluate everything for temporary reductions before fulltime personnel go out the door. People are the soul of any organization and should always be the last thing to cut.

- Once a reduction is decided on, initiate a process to review all individuals identified for release with a certain amount of experience and organizational tenure by the leadership team with an HR recommendation before releasing such persons. If cutting workers is the only option, employees with a history of things like poor performance, ethical lapses, or behavioral issues should be the first to go. Age, sex and race should never be a factor in identifying individuals for release.

Checklist

- ✓ Does HR use all available government compensation databases to determine pay bands for each type and category position?
- ✓ Are pay bands posted on the organization's website?
- ✓ Is there an HR process for annual reviews, and does it require clear, specific justification for the highest ratings?
- ✓ Is a quota system used for the highest ratings?
- ✓ Are bonuses represented as a percentage of annual pay, and is it the same for all personnel?

I have seen and been involved in too many layoffs and reductions-in-force to appreciate unrealistic rates of pay while good, highly dedicated people with unparalleled experience go out the door. Controlling labor rates is a crucial piece of the competition puzzle—all the way from the leadership team to the new college recruit or production technician. Although it is unwise to arbitrarily reduce an individual's salary, reducing the pay bands of vacant positions is a good start to lowering labor cost, especially at the senior management and leadership levels.

During longer-than-expected economic downturns, there are numerous options to decrease labor costs before a layoff is undertaken. Delay, reduce, or cancel training, travel, bonuses, monetary awards, and annual pay raises until business improves. Such moves will also help build employee confidence and cut replacement costs when business picks up.

STRATEGY 15

Ensure Customer Satisfaction

Customer satisfaction is a determining factor and the first of three essential components that keeps an organization in business; the other two are product quality and service quality. These three elements are what separate a great organization from an average one. The purpose of being in business is to make money by selling quality products or services to someone else. The more we sell, the more money we make. So why would anyone not want to make customer satisfaction a top priority? With aggressive competition from both domestic and foreign competitors, the need for everyone in the organization to take ownership of customer satisfaction is very real—especially when the additional cost is essentially zero.

Rules

- Keep customer satisfaction at the forefront.
- Connect the dots between product quality, superior service, satisfied customers, annual performance, and job security.
- Develop, maintain, and review customer-satisfaction measures at leadership meetings.
- Intervene anytime there is a customer issue that is not resolved promptly.
- Always treat customers with respect and professional courtesy.
- Answer customer concerns within twenty-four hours or sooner, or provide a status report if the issue is still open.

Key Points

1. Make customer satisfaction a top priority.
2. Maintain a world-class customer-satisfaction process.
3. Develop a matrix for measuring customer satisfaction.
4. Explore low-cost approaches to improve customer satisfaction.
5. Make it easy for customers to contact the organization.
6. Look for ways to save the customer money.

Discussion

1. Make customer satisfaction a top priority.

   It is paramount to keep customer satisfaction in front of everyone, every day, using the most effective communication methods. Connecting the dots between a quality product, customer satisfaction, sales volume, and job security will reinforce their importance and preclude message overload.

2. Maintain a world-class customer-satisfaction process.

   Maintain a proactive process that incorporates multiple approaches, subprocesses, and measures. Identifying customer-satisfaction focal points for organizational products and services will maintain control and ensure rapid response to potential problems. This method outlines responsibilities, establishes timelines, delineates documentation requirements, and tracks all customer issues until their resolution. The process should require the relevant focal point to review the resulting data file for lessons learned, product defects, etc.; update the management information system (MIS); and communicate any significant findings to the appropriate departments and the leadership team.

3. Develop a matrix for measuring quality and customer satisfaction.

   In no priority order or combination of data points, a matrix may include:

TWENTY-FIVE STRATEGIES FOR ORGANIZATIONAL SUCCESS

Customer	Product	Order Size	$ Value	Returns	$ Value
Customer	Order	Due Date	Del Date	Reason	
Customer	Order	Due Date	Order CNX	Reason	
Customer	Program	Budget	Date	Over	Under
Customer	New Orders	Due Date	On Budget	On Schedule	
New Customer	Order	Due Date	On Budget	On Schedule	
Total Sales	Weekly	Monthly	Quarterly	$ Value	Returns/ Reason
Service Calls	Initial	Returns			
Product	Average Total Sales $		Marketing Campaign		New Sales $

4. Explore low-cost approaches to improve customer satisfaction.

- Ensure customers know who to contact with a problem. While most retail businesses maintain a customer-service station, identify a real person and a phone number. It is far superior to a 1-800 number attached to an answering machine. If an answering machine is used, check it early each workday and contact customers promptly.
- Extend product warranties and use them as a selling point. Alternatively, offer a lower-cost extended warranty than your competitors.
- Use relevant data applications to track customer transactions to expedite returns, rebates, and warranty resolution.
- If practical, allow customers to rent or lease high-valued equipment with maintenance and service options.
- Host customer feedback lunches for high-volume customers
- Sponsor appreciation events to acquaint customers with new product lines.

5. Make it easy for customers to contact the organization.

- Place contact information and phone numbers on order receipts and delivery forms.
- For large-order repeat customers, assign a customer-satisfaction focal point.

6. Look for ways to save the customer money. These may include the following:

    - special discounts for larger orders
    - free delivery
    - free smooth-flow resupply or set delivery dates
    - free installation
    - free extended warranty
    - free marketing
    - free financing for specific periods
    - low financing rates
    - free or low-cost upgrades

Checklist

✓ Is the customer-satisfaction process current?
✓ Has a customer-satisfaction focal point been identified?
✓ Has contact information been posted and publicized?
✓ Has the focal point's personal cell number been provided to high-volume customers?

> Establishing a solid proactive customer-satisfaction process is easy. The basic concept is to use common sense and logic. Draw on your personal experience and put yourself in the customer's place. Is the product reliable and easy to install and operate? Does it perform as advertised? Is it easy to service? Are there any warranty problems? Happy customers will return, perform zero-cost advertising, and assist in generating new business.

STRATEGY 16

Make Quality a Top Priority

There is no substitute for producing and selling a high-quality sustainable product that requires little to no maintenance. While the product may have been built by one or more manufacturers, it's the name that goes on it that customers remember when they decide to purchase another. So why would anyone want to manufacture, or have manufactured, a so-so product when the same resources could be used to produce a high-quality item that increases market share and demands a higher price?

It takes less effort to sell a product with a name known for high-quality goods; such products sell themselves, as they bear the name of choice. Name-brand merchandise frequently gets free marketing support by exposure in public, industrial, and consumer publications. Without question, positive reviews increase sales, while negative reviews generate a good deal of additional costs as companies try to counter damaging examinations and ultimately lower the price of the item. Placing emphasis on first-time quality does work and can add appreciably to the bottom line

The same can be said about any organization that provides services as a business. If the company performs as advertised and provides superior service, it will do well. Otherwise, people will seek another company that delivers better results.

Rules

- Make first-time quality the organizational standard.
- Develop, maintain, and review quality measures at leadership meetings.
- Connect the dots between a quality product, superior service, satisfied customers, and job security.
- Customers will pay more for a product with a quality reputation.
- Intervene whenever there is a quality issue that is not resolved promptly.
- Always treat customers with quality issues with respect and professional courtesy.

Key Points

1. Make first-time quality the standard for production.
2. Review quality measures at leadership meetings.
3. Issue a warranty that exceeds the industry norm.
4. Maintain a very proactive continuous improvement (CI) process.
5. Maintain a process to capture customer feedback regarding product quality.
6. Connect the dots between a quality product, superior service, satisfied customers, and job security.
7. Use personal experiences in judging product quality.

Discussion

1. Make first-time quality the standard for production.
    - The overall first-time quality goal is to design and produce products that never break, require a recall, or function other than advertised. A first-time quality or "build it right the first time" approach reduces overhead as the number of returns, for whatever reason, decreases appreciably. Products that do not break or require an excessive amount of maintenance shout out when customers expand their business requirements.

- Quality is the one thing that separates great organizations from average organizations. In today's competitive market, quality is the determining factor that positions organizations to grow. Likewise, it is frequently a significant reason why organizations go under. Failing organizations will often blame things like the economy, foreign competition, labor costs, and energy costs; however, it is more likely that such organizations did not pay attention to the quality of their products or services.

2. Review quality measures at leadership meetings.

   The following list represents some items for periodic review at leadership team meetings that may warrant intervention:

   - unresolved product quality issues, including the date that the issue was identified, its status, and possible impact
   - quality issues with new products
   - product design issues that impact product quality
   - manufacturing processes producing quality problems
   - high return rates for various products
   - higher service problems with various products

3. Issue a warranty that exceeds the industry norm.

   Product warranties speak volumes and send a very powerful message to the customer regarding the quality of the product. The warranty should exceed the industry norm and be featured extensively in the product's marketing with a comparison to warranties offered by the competition. Why buy an item with a three-year warranty when you can get a comparably priced item with a four- or five-year warranty?

4. Maintain a very proactive continuous improvement (CI) process.

   - For purposes of this strategy, a CI process is an effort to reduce the number of parts in a product, the number of touch labor steps in building a product, or the hours required to complete a process or use electronic security over humans walking the floors, etc. Review each of the organization's processes annually for improvement and reduction in labor and material costs.

- A CI mind-set should be integrated into every facet of the organization to improve product quality—from design to manufacturing, to marketing, to delivery and installation, to servicing. Embed CI into every process, function, and management structure.

- Incorporate a CI process into the production cycle that encourages all personnel to identify improvements to the design or production process, which in turn could yield tremendous benefits in time, touch labor, and material costs. Reducing the number of parts in a product or the number of production steps without reducing quality will have a tremendous impact on production costs, pricing, and profit margins. Integrating advances in technology can also improve quality while reducing costs.

- Constantly challenge design and manufacturing personnel to look for better ways of fabricating a high-quality product with fewer, stronger, and lighter parts. The result is to make a product that raises the bar on quality, functionality, and return on investment.

5. Maintain a process to capture customer feedback regarding product quality.

    Depending on the product, develop multiple methods to capture customer feedback regarding the design, utility, performance, and any other important product characteristics. Such methods could include product reviews, displays, personal invitations, product demonstrations, written surveys, and third-party technology shows.

6. Connect the dots between a quality product, superior service, satisfied customers, and job security.

It is important that all personnel understand the connection between the organization's products and services with quality, customer satisfaction, organizational performance, and job security. Such communications put everything into perspective and serve as a subtle reminder of where the funds for their paychecks come from.

7. Use personal experiences in judging product quality.

- Use your buying experiences for various personal items to judge the quality of your products. Would you keep buying something that routinely breaks down, falls apart, or just does not work as advertised? Would you continue to select vehicles that require frequent maintenance?

- Use your personal experiences to judge excellent quality service. Start with restaurants you frequent. Why do you like them? Is it the food, ambiance, service, or prices? More than likely, it is a combination of all factors. Does one attribute surpass the others?

Checklist

✓ Are all quality processes current?
✓ Are first-time quality benefits communicated?
✓ Has a customer quality focal point been identified?
✓ Has contact information been posted and publicized?
✓ Are individuals and teams recognized for identifying quality improvements?
✓ Are quality initiatives measured to determine which ones produce the best results?

Quality is the cornerstone for any business organization. It is a powerful mind-set that can be contagious throughout the organization, providing the leadership team gives it the attention it warrants. Producing a quality product gives team members a sense of pride and ownership that benefits everyone, all the time. Quality is the product of a steady CI emphasis. Connecting the dots will go far in getting the workforce to participate actively in improving product quality and service. Customers will pay more for a product or service that has a proven record for quality.

In order to instill quality as priority one, I would discuss quality issues and CI ideas frequently at staff and all-hands meetings. Another essential practice is to post visible quality measures that speak for themselves, such as measures based on customer feedback, statistics, and historical data comparing what was "then" to what exists "now."

STRATEGY 17

Establish a Process-Management System

Process management is a concept that promotes the use of defined, continuously updated procedures to reduce non-value-added costs associated with labor and materials. It fine-tunes the organization's operations to manufacture products more efficiently, to include the way we sell them and the way we support our customers in servicing them. In short, process management is continuous improvement in motion.

Rules

- Establish a proactive process-management system to identify and remove non-value-added steps in designing, manufacturing, selling, installing, and servicing products.
- Monitor process management activities via the management information system (MIS).

Key Points

1. Process management is one of the most effective management tools available to reduce costs.
2. Processes directly influence the quality of products and services.

3. Each process must have an owner.
4. Make each process simple, short, and concise.
5. There are numerous ways to improve any given process.

Discussion

1. Process management is one of the most effective management tools available to reduce costs.

   - A process is a way we conduct business, hire people, buy supplies, design products, manufacture goods, market products, handle customer complaints, and deliver merchandise. A process is also the way we plan, conduct training, protect our proprietary information, and perform financial audits. Each process represents either overhead or a direct-charge program cost. Short, simple, less complex processes tend to generate more compliance and keep costs lower. Processes that are more intricate are apt to be reviewed less often due to their complexity.

   - An organizational process review allows management and functional process owners to look at those processes that keep the organization operating. The goal is to identify and eliminate non-value-added steps, with zero impact on the purpose or function of the process.

   - Many organizations have electronic systems that allow individuals to complete various reporting, financial, and work-related tasks online for management review and approval. These computerized databases allow faster input and retrieval while providing greater storage with minimum space. Such processes reduce paperwork and the corresponding number of man-hours to keep the paperwork moving through the management chain.

   - Costs savings occur each time a process update eliminates or allows a greater use of technology to decrease touch labor requirements. Product process reviews encourage the use of newer, lighter, stronger materials, as well as advances in technology to reduce the number of parts, size, or design limitations. Such reviews can introduce ideas and concepts from competitor products—all of which may reduce costs while increasing the operational performance capability of the product.

2. Processes directly influence the quality of products and services.

- A technical process review allows designers, engineers, fabricators, and test experts an opportunity to identify ways to improve the quality of any aspect of a system, subsystem, product design, or manufacture. Reviews allow specialists to look at the smallest component or the overall system to improve capabilities and enhance operational performance.

- Including production-line personnel in technical discussions can produce out-of-the-box thinking on ways to improve the manufacturing process and overall quality, performance, and serviceability of the product.

- Inviting customers to participate in reviews can also add a new dimension to product utility and maintainability.

3. Each process must have an owner.

- The role of the owner is to make sure that their processes are maintained, updated, and published. More importantly, the owner must ensure that each process is current and reflects all organizational requirements necessary to accomplish a particular task, such as expense-report processing, new personnel hires, prototype fabrication, or product testing. Process owners are also responsible for incorporating customer and government requirements into applicable processes per contractual requirements.

- In large functional and line organizations, there are multiple process owners, as they are identified by task, job, or requirement.

4. Make each process simple, short, and concise.

    - The best-written processes are those prepared by the process owners based on input from the individuals who perform the task or work. These are the people who have the greatest understanding as to what actions must be taken to accomplish a given job, the order of each action, the precision of each operation, and whether any latitude exists.

    - Construct each written process to be simple, short, and to the point. A simple step process usually works well. Incorporate graphics and artwork to enhance understanding, especially for individuals who are more visually oriented. Anyone who hooks up multiple electronic devices or has ever put together a child's toy can follow a step process.

    - Among the many rewards associated with a well-written process is the capacity to train new personnel faster and the ability to move personnel between similar jobs. An additional benefit comes when new personnel question certain steps that may be unnecessary.

5. There are numerous ways to improve any given process.

    - The best way to determine what works and what doesn't in a process is to ask the individuals who perform the task as part of their job.

    - Have the individuals participate in technical process reviews.

    - Bring together a cross section of personnel to review organizational processes.

    - Customer audits and or inspections frequently spot process improvement areas and suggestions for enhancements.

    - Membership in various national associations may identify world-class or best practices to incorporate into current organizational processes.

Checklist

- ✓ Has every process, procedure, or task that requires man-hours to complete been documented?
- ✓ Does each process have an owner?
- ✓ Is each process periodically reviewed by those working the task to eliminate non-value-added steps?
- ✓ Is each process simple, short, and easy to understand?
- ✓ Is there a process to measure and document the cost savings and/or cost reductions of improvements generated by updated processes?

> Process management is one of the most inexpensive, cost-effective tools we can incorporate into our operations. It offers a mechanism for identifying and reducing material and labor costs, while keeping the organization lean and the profit margin greater.
>
> While assigned to a major aircraft-development project, I was asked to downsize my staff as part of a bigger cost-reduction initiative. Even though the workload was growing and there was no decline in the scope of our responsibilities, we reduced the impact to the team by constantly looking at our processes to eliminate non-value-added steps. We kept close contact with our customers to ensure that all of their requirements were satisfied.

STRATEGY 18

Engage in Program Management

For the most part, program management is a mirror image of functional management, except that this strategy provides labor resources to the program to accomplish a particular task or contract. Such a task could involve thousands of dollars and hundreds of employees to develop a new computer application or security sensor. On the other hand, the program might involve billions of dollars, thousands of personnel, and years to complete, such as designing, building, and testing a new aircraft, boat, or satellite. Whatever the activity, resources are allocated to the program for a specific product with detailed specifications or capabilities by a designated date and budget.

Rules

- Recognize that program management requires a more micromanaging style of leadership.
- Hold daily meetings with all key personnel to ensure timely communication flow.
- Measure everything that requires labor and material expenditures.
- Monitor supplier activity closely.
- Never, ever assume; always follow up.

Key Points

1. The first rule of program management is to deliver a quality product on time, within budget, and as contracted.
2. Program management skill sets are very similar to those of an organizational team, with several significant exceptions.
3. Big programs produce many more challenges.
4. The right approach can help mitigate program challenges.

Discussion

1. The first rule of program management is to deliver a quality product on time, within budget, and as contracted.

   - This is the reason a micromanagement style of leadership is necessary. It's a fine line to navigate—avoid being intrusive into daily decision-making while closely monitoring all activities for potential problems and issues that could have a ripple effect throughout major parts of the program. It is essential to identify and resolve any concerns quickly to preclude bigger, more costly troubles. Get-well plans may be necessary to address any given issue.

   - Establish a dynamic, compartmentalized matrix system that measures progress on all key program components and immediately highlights any deviations or issues.

   - A wise move is to set up a restricted program information center. Similar to a military combat information hub, the center allows senior leaders and managers to visually review all key program activities in minutes, which can be vital if rapid intervention is needed.

   - When millions or billions of dollars are at risk, a strong proprietary and/or program security infrastructure will reduce the possibility of compromise. The contracting government agency will provide additional security guidance for any classified program.

2. Program management skill sets are very similar to an organizational team, with several significant exceptions.

Although a program requires its leaders and managers to have additional skill sets, it is important to assign or recruit individuals who have program management experience and a successful track record. In addition to their leadership and management ability, they must be able to lead and work with, in some situations, very difficult individuals and suppliers with poor reputations. A large program should not be used as a training ground. Exceptions include the need to:

- Micromanage all major program component activities.
- Identify program milestones to measure program progress.
- Foster and encourage an out-of-box, leapfrogging mind-set.
- Push the envelope to find solutions to challenges.
- Implement an unparalleled sense of urgency.
- Establish a steadfast fiscal discipline.
- Keep processes as simple as possible.
- Incorporate security in all decisions.

3. Big programs produce many more challenges.

The pitfalls associated with a large program involving internal and external organizations are many and varied. Success or failure is oftentimes dependent on factors like external suppliers, uncontrollable timetables, and delivery and quality promises that may not be achievable due to unforeseen circumstances. Programs that incorporate new or advanced technologies add a multitude of challenges. Second- and third-tier suppliers add their own set of challenges. Be prepared to implement a back-up plan to bring on a new supplier should a current supplier identify problems that could adversely impact costs and schedules.

4. The right approach can help mitigate program challenges.
   - Recruit leadership-team members who have the experience and proven track record for success. It is not the time or place to train someone new to program management.

- Timely information flow is critical for all players. The more dynamic the program, the greater the need for continual information flow.
  - Meet daily or as required with key personnel.
  - If appropriate, use teleconferencing, face time, or other methods to communicate with first-, second-, and even third-tier suppliers. Encryption may be required.
- Implement a network of departmental "tiger teams" that can respond quickly to specific challenges within their discipline. Identifying a controlled area with technical (computer and communications) and administrative support resources can expedite tiger team performance and ability to resolve the issue.
- Identify internal and external subject-matter experts for rapid response.

Checklist

✓ Are organizational processes in place to start up and support a new high-cost program?
✓ Are processes in place for identifying and assigning experienced personnel with the required skill sets to a new program?
✓ Have a restricted area and support equipment, etc., been identified for the program?
✓ Has a proprietary management information system been identified or set up to support the program?
✓ Is a dedicated security team required?

No matter the funding level for any given program, the principles for managing the program are akin to leading and managing an entire organization or enterprise. Some programs may be a mirror image of a much larger organization, while others may use part-time assignees, shared space, laboratories, AIS systems, test facilities, and fabrication shops. For any program launching a new design, system, or capability, the prospect of costs overruns is a major challenge due to the number of unknowns, unproven assumptions, new technology, or subcontractors overestimating their capabilities.

Therefore, close oversight—including a multitude of measures and communications—is most critical for success. Intervention by the leadership team is necessary whenever a significant organization program involving millions of dollars goes into an over-budget mode for any length of time without an implemented get-well plan. I have seen too many programs suffer due to inept managers not doing their job before customers pulled the funding plug.

STRATEGY 19

Control Overhead

An inability to control overhead costs is one of the primary reasons businesses fail. Although overhead costs increase with growth, the ability to absorb these expenses is much easier for larger organizations. The impact on smaller companies is more dramatic, as it makes their charge rates or prices less competitive. The challenge is to closely monitor all overhead for non-value-added costs, as they can quickly get out of control and adversely impact the company's ability to win new contracts or set new rates and prices.

Rules

- Maintain processes that monitor, track and highlight anomalies in overhead costs.
- Include overhead cost projections, timelines, rate impact, and contingency exit plans in all business strategies, non-core business initiatives, and expansion plans.
- Be prepared to close down failing non-core business initiatives that exceed budget, break deadlines, or do not meet basic return-on-investment expectations.
- Never assume. Always follow up.

Key Points

1. Evaluate each growth decision against time, investment, value, and payoff.

2. Reduce overhead costs for the following categories:
   - facility
   - power
   - physical security
   - personnel
   - research, development, test, and evaluation (RDT&E)
   - medical
   - other

3. Require leadership-team members to take control and ownership of their overhead costs.

Discussion

1. Evaluate each growth decision against time, investment, value, and payoff.

   - Core expansion decisions are often based on a number of industry and organizational projections and inputs that suggest growth, direction, and profitability opportunities. Growing the company without jeopardizing the organization's credit rating or debt load requires wise leadership decisions. After a decision, the need to manage all expansion costs for overruns or unforeseen events is paramount to avoid a major catastrophe.

   - Consider pre-planning responses to various contingency scenarios. Issuing contracts that require vendors to meet specific milestones on or by specific dates is critical. Such contractual requirements should include different levels of flexibility to create a win-win situation for everyone involved.

- The leadership team should not award an expansion contract to any company formed by several companies to compete for the contract. In such arrangements, responsibility and accountability frequently get lost in the contract's language and may result in slipped completion dates, significant cost increase, and potential lawsuits.

- Study each customer request for proposal (RFP) or proposal invitation for additional overhead costs. The leadership team must consider all projected costs and any customer cost-sharing against the length of the contract and potential benefits. Ask the following questions:

  o Does the RFP require an immediate turnkey operation or provide time and funds for organizational facility upgrades to meet the requirements of the contract?

  o Under what conditions can a customer pull out of the contract? Are they fiscally responsible for regulatory obligations to increase capabilities?

  o Will winning the contract require the organization to enlarge the workforce—in particular with skills that it does not normally employ?

  o Does the contract require all personnel be vetted or receive a government clearance?

  o Does the contract require the organization to seek other partners or subcontractors?

  o Would all expansion costs for the contract be a direct charge to the contract?

  o Are there opportunities for new contract add-ons?

  o Could the contract open doors or introduce the organization to new customers, partnerships, or joint ventures?

2. Reduce overhead costs for the following categories:
   - Facility
     - When planning a new facility, it may be wise to build it larger with the intent of renting space to reduce projected costs.
     - Although the trend is to replace organizational facility maintenance teams with outside vendors, this often backfires and increases installation maintenance costs. Having an in-house team that knows and understands the facility's challenges can preclude large, unnecessary expenditures. Internal teams frequently have multiple skill sets that allow them to correct a multitude of problems versus an outside contractor, such as a plumber or electrician.
     - Whether housing the organization in a hundred-year-old building or a newer facility, there are countless new products available to update walls, electrical systems, plumbing, lighting, heating, and cooling that can reduce noise, power consumption, and maintainability.
     - Software programs can assist in modifying work area layouts to improve work conditions while decreasing lighting, heating, and cooling costs.
     - Before a decision is made to expand floor space, consider employing a twenty-four-hour, multi-shift operation.
     - Identify functions that can be performed at employee homes, such as administrative, personnel, financial, and even some security functions. These types of arrangements can reduce floor-space requirements and associated costs.
     - Include designs in new facility plans that might allow the organization to expand and/or move various operations with minimum effort or expense—for example,

easily movable walls and areas that could be rented out until space is needed.

- Direct-charge government contracts may require that their assigned facilities be modified under very specific guidelines to provide greater control and security. Depending on the requirements, it may be more cost-effective to build such a facility than to modify an existing one.

- Power

  Most local power suppliers will perform an assessment to reduce power consumption. Frequently, their recommendations regarding savings can be accomplished with little expense.

- Physical Security

  - Maintaining a safe, secure working environment is paramount. Reducing the number of entry points and controlling entry via electronic ID cards is inexpensive as compared to threats posed by an unauthorized hostile entry. Restricting access to proprietary areas as well as computer centers is required to protect the organization's trade secrets. The use of video cameras throughout the facility and its grounds represents an effective, inexpensive deterrent.

  - Keeping a proprietary guard force may be required for those organizations that perform classified work for the government or another contractor. For companies that invest millions in RDT&E activities, a guard force is highly advised.

  - While the retail industry wants locations with easy access and high traffic volume, other service organizations can reduce physical security costs by just locating themselves on the third or fourth floor of a multistory building.

- Personnel

    Having a workforce split between full-time, part-time, and contractors allows the organization to quickly respond to new contract spikes, as well as downsize due to economic conditions. Placing highly skilled individuals on retainer could encourage the government to grant security clearances to allow their participation on contracts without any break for access processing.

- RDT&E

    Organizations that have an RDT&E capability fully understand the associated costs. Facilities and personnel represent a significant cost to the business, especially when their activities are not always included in new products or contracts. Forming joint ventures with other organizations, academia, and various government agencies can reduce the costs and risks to everyone.

- Medical

    Many large business campuses with numerous operations maintain an onsite clinic to provide emergency medical support or response. Smaller organizations typically depend on their medical plans or have an arrangement with a local clinic or hospital to provide medical assistance. Both provisions may reduce overall medical costs to the organization and its personnel.

- Other

    Numerous other jobs and requirements increase an organization's overhead costs. Functions like marketing, training, and administration have their own skilled personnel. Requirements likes travel, transportation, supplies, furniture, computer systems, communications, etc., all add overhead costs. As stated above, all of these expenses need to be tracked and monitored for non-value-added reductions.

3. Require leadership-team members to take control and ownership of their overhead costs.

Requiring leadership-team members to involve their direct reports in controlling overhead costs will increase ownership throughout the organization and maximize resource allocation, utilization, and costs avoidance. The goal is not to reduce the workforce, but to ensure that the labor force performs value-added tasks that contribute to organizational success. Making overhead reductions an annual performance measure for the leadership team as well as their direct reports would be a useful start.

Checklist

✓ Are policies, processes, and performance measures in place to track and monitor organizational overhead costs?
✓ Are processes simple and easy to follow and accomplish?
✓ Are performance measures being discussed at leadership-team meetings?
✓ Are individuals and teams acknowledged and rewarded for finding areas to cut costs?

> Continued organizational success is tied to a company's ability to manage overhead costs. When costs are controlled, the organization is better equipped to absorb lost contracts, delayed contracts, disruption in customer payments, late supplier deliveries, and other events that add stress to cash flow. Having participated in multiple reduction-in-force (RIF) events, I have a good idea of the things that can go wrong. I saw too many dedicated people go out the door. Although our HR team did a fantastic job in helping individuals find employment elsewhere, each RIF communicated a very negative message to those remaining.

> No one can understand the stress, pain, and disappointment of being let go until they receive a pink slip themselves. Although customer decisions played a role, existing overhead rates exacerbated overall financial conditions to an extent that drastic action was required. Leadership teams must monitor overhead costs and interject themselves when activities, programs, or new initiatives go over budget.

STRATEGY 20

Protect Proprietary Information

Over four decades ago, the FBI became very concerned about the number of foreign attempts to steal not only US government secrets but also business trade secrets and proprietary information. Since then, the threat has grown considerably, and the resources to prevent it have not kept up.

Fast forward to today. The foreign threat is much more aggressive and multidirectional, with no business that makes and sells products—or provides services—exempt or safe. Although China has increased its purchase of US businesses, it continues to steal as much as it can. A vast majority of economic espionage events are attributed to China. Although computer hacking may be preferred, high-value individuals with access to critical information are frequently targeted. The Chinese will also recruit Chinese personnel who have families in China, recruit someone else who has access and knowledge of the targeted organization, and even insert a trained operative if the information is crucial. The FBI puts the total loss to US business interests at tens of billions dollars a year, and thousands of jobs are lost due to trade-secret theft.

Any business involved in the research and development of new products, software, chemicals, or anything that gives the organization an edge over the competition should maintain a very proactive proprietary security program. Such information is the organization's lifeblood. The theft of trade secrets is alive and well. It can ruin any company that does not have processes in place to counter such threats.

(Note: Readers are encouraged to go to the Justice Department and FBI websites for more detailed information regarding Chinese and other foreign economic intelligence activities.)

Rules

- Never assume that an organization's trade secrets are completely safe.
- Make proprietary security everyone's responsibility.
- Connect the dots between proprietary security and keeping the doors open.
- Compartmentalize programs, proprietary activities, and their supporting computer systems.
- Maintain and actively support a professional security team.
- Restrict sensitive research to full-time organizational personnel.
- Maintain communications with applicable US government agencies regarding foreign industrial espionage activity near organizational facility locations.

Key Points

1. Realize that industrial espionage is alive and well, and frequently multidirectional.
2. Integrate proprietary security into all aspects of an organization's business operations.
3. Identify all organizational information that requires protection.
4. Establish and maintain a simple, effective security program.
5. Look for measures that cost very little to protect proprietary information.

Discussion

1. Realize that industrial espionage is alive and well, and frequently multidirectional.

   - Anyone who researches and creates new technology, materials, drugs, and software—or reengineers old technology—is a target for domestic and foreign competition, foreign governments, professional hackers, and information peddlers. Any organization with research as a core business element or plans to compete for government contracts should take proprietary security very seriously. Within the military industrial complex, that which is considered to be proprietary one day can very well be classified the next by a government customer.

   - China, Russia, and several other countries fully appreciate the benefit of stealing trade secrets, as it saves millions if not billions in RDT&E (research, development, test, and evaluation) costs. The ROI (return on investment) for such countries to retain a state-supported cyber-spying community to acquire information is tremendous. It also provides the capability to initiate information warfare attacks when they so desire. Cyber-security espionage news is becoming too commonplace not to take action. Just one incident of a compromised database can be a disaster internally and within an organization's customer base. Some corporations and financial institutions elect not to report such penetrations due to projected business loss and impact to their reputation.

   - Land and space-based assets continue to intercept business communications and other signals.

   - Inserting an operative into a target organization can be expensive, but very rewarding. Hiring someone on the inside who already knows the organization's security measures is easier and cheaper. It is often not that hard to find someone who has been passed over for promotion, been disciplined, or has money or relationship problems. While blackmail is used to recruit some high-value individuals, it requires more time and resources, and it can get messy.

- The FBI continues to be very effective in catching domestic and foreign operatives, but it does not have the resources to degrade foreign activity appreciably. While failures to prevent foreign espionage get a great deal of press, success stories get very little to protect sources and methods.

- Government agencies, including the FBI, are always willing to help organizations understand the foreign threat in their area. As previously discussed, the Chinese continue a very aggressive collection campaign on the US West Coast by recruiting legal émigrés who have family in China.

2. Integrate proprietary security into all aspects of an organization's business operations.

- New employee training should address proprietary security measures, which need to be very visible, easily understood, and simple to carry out. Hold briefings on security requirements several times during the year and have attendees sign a log to indicate compliance.

- Make sure all organizational paper and electronic communications have appropriate markings and any required cover sheets.

- Assign different levels of protection to the various categories of information. Each level may include the use of page markings and cover sheets that carry instructions for controlling, transmitting, and storing the information when not in use.

- Use visuals throughout the organization to identify the categories of information that require protection and how they are to be protected.

3. Identify all organizational information that requires protection. Identify and protect all information that makes the organization competitive and successful. This information, if disclosed, would give competitors the upper hand in winning contracts, new customers, and current clients, thus driving the company out of business. Such information may include the following:

   o computer code
   o product design, fabrication techniques, test data
   o prototype development and tests
   o system integration technologies, subsystem designs
   o proprietary software, applications
   o new, lighter, stronger materials
   o miniaturization, nanotechnology
   o formulas, chemical compound recipes
   o new advanced production and manufacturing processes
   o internally modified production equipment
   o reverse-engineering findings
   o solicited and unsolicited customer proposals, pricing
   o personnel information and compensation
   o customer lists, customer requirements, and timelines
   o supplier information and costs
   o promotion and sales strategies, timelines
   o joint ventures, new acquisitions, business expansions
   o sensitive organizational relationships

4. Establish and maintain a simple, effective security program. Such a program should include the following:

   - Administrative security

     o Establish processes to mark, transmit (by mail and electronically), and control proprietary or trade-secret information. It would be prudent to have the legal department review all processes and cover-sheet instructions to determine if the procedures would stand up in a court of law.

- Information security

    o Establish processes to identify information that you do not want the competition to know. There should be no question in anyone's mind as to what organizational data is proprietary—notably, trade-secret information that is not communicated outside the organization or with non-organizational personnel.

- Personnel security

    o Establish processes to create nondisclosure employee contracts, vet applicants, issue ID and access control cards, maintain personnel files, and submit nomination packages for government approvals. Employee contracts should be ironclad and able to withstand any court review to protect trade-secret information for life—should an individual leave to join the competition.

- Physical security

    o Establish processes and access control systems for entry to and exit from the facility, as well as access control for areas within the facility. Lighting, cameras, and a proprietary guard force would substantially enhance any physical security program.

- Technical security

    o Establish processes and ground rules for maintaining current and projected computer systems, LANs, WANs, central computer facilities, stand-alone computer facilities, any external connectivity, and encrypted communication capability. Stand-alone computer systems that have no connectivity outside their area or room offer a very high level of security for the data stored and processed. Computer transfer files are virus-checked before input into a stand-alone system.

- Program security
    - o Establish security processes to protect organizational and customer information per contract requirements.
- Security education
    - o Develop and conduct periodic security training to increase awareness of individual responsibility and organizational processes to protect proprietary and customer information. Inviting government security professionals to participate will enhance any training.

5. Look for measures that cost very little to protect proprietary information.

- Include a section in each individual's application or employee contract that prohibits the disclosure of any organization information to an unauthorized individual. An nondisclosure agreement (NDA) may also be necessary.

- If applicable, frequently remind personnel of the organization's policy that all work areas and personal containers are subject to unannounced inspection by security personnel to insure safety, information protection, and possible government compliance.

- Have security guards perform unannounced purse and briefcase inspections.

- Give security personnel the authority to stop and inspect an individual's containers and automobile while on organization property.

- Maintain a 1-800 number for people who wish to report a possible security incident without identifying themselves. Call-in numbers cannot be recorded or traceable for this to work.

- As a rule, no individual should be allowed to take trade-secret or proprietary information out of the facility. When necessary and authorized, identify and have the individual sign for trade-secret information taken out of the facility.

- Incorporate a family of stand-alone computer systems to house specific disciplines of proprietary or program information.

- Trade-secret information, proposal strategies or organizational plans should never ever be discussed during air travel or in a foreign hotel that caters to Americans. Some foreign governments electronically monitor Americans staying in selected hotels. There have been situations wherein foreign operatives have entered hotel rooms to review the contents of a traveler's briefcase, laptop, and other electronic devices.

- Issue encrypted communication devices to individuals who are involved in creating and managing trade-secret or proprietary information. Make such devices a requirement when such individuals travel.

- Do not allow part-timers, contractors, or students to work on any sensitive proprietary program or data. SME consultants who have signed an NDA and have a history with the organization would be an exception.

Checklist

- ✓ Do professionally trained individuals staff the security team?
- ✓ Have organizational security processes and supporting documentation (employee contracts, NDAs, cover sheets, etc.) been documented, reviewed by legal, and publicized?
- ✓ Is a proactive, multifaceted security training program in place and operational?
- ✓ Have proprietary and trade-secret information, data files, and devices been identified?
- ✓ Is the security program being actively supported by the leadership and management teams?
- ✓ Is program security meeting the security requirements and expectations of its customers?

Most of my working life was split between the intelligence and special-security communities. I devoted numerous days to developing and orchestrating various collection activities or protecting our operations, research, and development programs from foreign efforts. It is extremely important that security teams are staffed with multidiscipline professionals who understand the threats and what measures are necessary to counter them.

The military and other government security and intelligence agencies offer industry a tremendous asset that can be tapped for experienced individuals. Cybersecurity professionals would significantly enhance any security team to counter the ever-increasing multifaceted, multidirectional foreign electronic threat. The Justice Department is just one of several agencies that maintains an excellent website.

Security is one profession that measures success in negative numbers; zero computer breaches, zero information compromises, zero unauthorized trade secret disclosures, and zero unauthorized facility entries. Like quality and customer satisfaction, all personnel must take ownership for protecting proprietary information. Connecting the dots between good security and keeping the doors open is appropriate!

STRATEGY 21

Use Strategic Planning

A strategic-planning process can do a myriad of tasks for an organization, as it helps to define a strategy, provide direction, and allocate resources to pursue its plan. The leadership team can employ the process to decide what, where, when, and how it is going to achieve multiyear goals and objectives. Planning compels players to think of their current resources—that is, what they will need, when and where they will need it, and how it will be used. Each time the plan is reviewed, team members can include the most recent innovations in technology, essential skills, customer demands, economic conditions, anomalies, and cost of money.

Rules

- Strategic plans focus on the future.
- Strategic plans provide direction, application, resource projection, and timelines.
- Strategic plans are a reality check as to where the organization is and where it wants to be, when, and what it will take to get there.
- Strategic plans send a positive message to all organizational stakeholders.

Key Points

1. Strategic planning benefits everyone.
2. Strategic planning adds direction and focus to the organization.
3. Strategic planning encourages and facilitates out-of-the-box thinking.
4. Consider specific items during the planning process.

Discussion

1. Strategic planning benefits everyone.

    A strategic-planning process allows the leadership team to focus on the future and offers valuable information to investors, bankers, and stockholders. Within the transportation industry, planning for an electric car and now a driverless auto must have started years ago to get where they are today. The same type of futuristic planning is applicable to most organizations.

2. Strategic planning adds direction and focus to the organization.

    A great deal of industrial and government research is reviewed and questioned before the leadership team makes a decision regarding the future direction of the organization. Whether the decision involves new product lines, leapfrog technology, or modifying current products, it provides direction and focus. It allows the organization to target its resources and creativity toward reaching plan milestones.

3. Strategic planning encourages and facilitates out-of-the-box thinking.

    For decades, the US has suffered from an onslaught of goods produced by cheap foreign labor. Personnel involved in the strategic planning process are encouraged to maximize the use of all applicable technologies—including manufacturing processes and advanced materials—to create and sell products at a lower cost and faster than foreign competition. Any planning should make it clear that those individuals displaced by newer technology will be trained or cross-trained into new job classifications at or above their current wage level.

4. Consider specific items during the planning process:
    - new facility requirements
    - available labor pools and skill requirements
    - city, state, and federal tax incentives
    - technology advances
    - advanced manufacturing equipment and processes
    - new materials (such as composites)
    - miniaturization and nanotechnology
    - available power and natural resources

Checklist

✓ Does a strategic-planning process exist?
✓ Is the planning team manned with professional planners?
✓ What timelines have been identified to develop, review, approve, and publish the strategic plan?

> The benefits of a strategic plan far outweigh the energy and hours it takes to develop one. A good plan forces people to think outside the box, reach a consensus, and get their ducks in a row. The airline and auto industries are excellent examples of an in-depth strategic planning process based on customer projections, technology, tooling, facility costs, and profit forecasts.

STRATEGY 22

Plan for Contingencies

Before any discussion on contingency planning takes place, note that the organization's primary goal in an emergency is to protect the lives of its personnel. That said, preparing for possible contingencies is just good business practice. Not only can planning save lives, it can potentially avert thousands, if not millions, of dollars in lost assets and revenue for a business.

Why would a business *not* have a contingency plan if it is located in a flood plain, on the Gulf Coast, in tornado alley, or perhaps in a heavily wooded area with a history of forest fires? What about organizations that have had their (a) computer systems hacked, (b) files stolen, or (c) computers contaminated with a virus? Any organization can be the target of a bomb threat or a disgruntled employee with a gun. Losses from any scenario can be lessened with a planned response in place.

Although not discussed in this strategy, organizations with union employees should develop plans to implement upon an unanticipated walkout or work stoppage.

Rules

- Plans should be short and very direct.
- Plans should define a purpose, delegate responsibilities, establish timelines, and outline responses.

Key Points

1. The most significant benefit of pre-planning is to coach all organizational players regarding their responses before an event happens.
2. The leadership team is the final approving authority for all plans.
3. Organizational subunits should include addendums that further define their responsibilities, responses, and timelines.
4. The leadership team and key players should hold event exercises to understand their responsibilities and possible glitches.
5. Discuss plan overviews periodically during all-hands meetings and highlight them on the organization's website.
6. New-employee indoctrinations should discuss plans and where they can be reviewed.

Discussion

1. The most significant benefit of pre-planning is to coach all organizational players regarding their responses before an event happens.

    Plans require the leadership team to think through possible scenarios and identify the most effective response. Checklists are helpful in identifying actions to complete, the order of completion, and time needed. While protecting personnel is always the top priority, maintaining communication is also key. Prepositioning resources may be required to facilitate response time. Participating in local and medical response exercises would provide greater insight.

2. The leadership team is the final approving authority for all plans.

    The leadership team should critically review each strategy to ensure that it is realistic and accomplishes its purpose.

3. Organization subunits should include addendums that further define their responsibilities, responses, and timelines. Subunits include the following:

   - facilities
   - security
   - information technology
   - human resources

4. The leadership team and key players should hold event exercises to understand their responsibilities and possible glitches.

   Leadership-team members need an all-inclusive understanding of their responsibilities, roles, and timelines, as well as an awareness of the responsibilities of other key personnel.

5. Discuss plan overviews periodically during all-hands meetings and highlight them on the organization's website.

   All individuals need to know when and how to respond to an anticipated event or one taking place. Post highly visible signs and posters throughout the facility to serve as a reminder. Cover plan overviews quarterly and especially during specific seasons for tornados, hurricanes, and the like.

6. New-employee indoctrinations should discuss the plans and where they can be reviewed.

   New employees should know that such plans exist. Providing new hires with a response checklist of the plans in the welcoming packet would be a plus.

Checklist

- ✓ Have plans been prepared and approved for all possible contingencies?
- ✓ Has each plan been discussed at leadership-team meetings?
- ✓ Have plan overviews been briefed at all-hands assemblies?

- ✓ Does the organization's website have a section devoted to emergency plans?
- ✓ Have signs and instructions been posted throughout the organization?
- ✓ Has a restricted area been set aside to serve as a crisis management center?

> Contingency planning is easy and cost-effective to implement. All key people need to think through the actions necessary to respond to a natural or manmade emergency. Planning identifies who will do what and when they will do it. Such pre-thinking has the potential to save lives and thousands or even millions of dollars in lost or damaged resources. Although some emergencies provide an appreciable amount of warning—such as rising water and flooding—others, such as tornadoes, provide very little.

STRATEGY 23

Form Business Alliances

The practice of forming business alliances is an excellent alternative to acquiring competitor organizations. Some of America's leading industrial captains have stated that purchasing a competitor can fall appreciably short due to significant cultural differences, where the resulting costs would far outweigh the wisdom behind the acquisition. Many organizations form alliances to grow their business while openly utilizing the other's capabilities, assets, and talents. Such associations offer opportunities to expand into new business areas, increase customer base, and minimize risks. Unlike partnerships, alliances allow greater flexibility—including withdrawal.

Rules

- Always consider a business alliance when the business opportunity far outweighs the downside.
- Thoroughly investigate the organization and its leadership team.
- Hire an experienced consultant who understands the positives, negatives, and potential pitfalls of a business alliance.
- Ensure all documentation clearly and legally outlines the purpose, roles, responsibilities, cost sharing, asset utilization, ground rules, liabilities—to protect both companies and to facilitate an exit strategy if the alliance must be dissolved.
- Never assume. Get it in writing!

Key Points

1. Thoroughly vet the organization and its leadership team.
2. Keep an open mind, and form alliances that make good business sense.
3. Fully understand the opportunities and pitfalls associated with each potential alliance.
4. Have the finance team run the numbers for each possible scenario.

Discussion

1. Thoroughly vet the organization and its leadership team.

   Ensure the organization and leadership team are fully vetted before any legal arrangements are made. Unanticipated surprises can add excessive costs and do more damage than any potential upside in an alliance. Vetting should identify ownership, financial status, lawsuits, labor issues, customer complaints, and reputation for quality.

2. Keep an open mind, and form alliances that make good business sense.

   Alliances allow an organization without the capabilities and assets needed to fulfill the requirements of a contract an opportunity to bid on the contract, as either the prime or a subcontractor. These agreements open new doors to expand the customer base and build a reputation in a new business arena.

3. Fully understand the opportunities and pitfalls associated with each potential alliance.

   Before vetting potential alliance players, have an experienced consultant highlight the positives, negatives, and lessons learned from an alliance that succeeded and those that failed, and the reasons for failure. Employ internal and external sources to check potential players, visit their facilities, and hold open discussions between those work centers and the departments affected. Not doing this could open a can of expensive worms that no organization wants.

4. Have the finance team run the numbers for each possible scenario.

    Is the decision to form an alliance worth the risk, based on the best ROI (return on investment) projections the finance team can determine? Understanding this financial data will allow the leadership team to balance the potential upside of new business opportunities against a weak or zero ROI.

Checklist

✓ Has a process been prepared to identify the possibilities and benefits of forming various alliances to enhance core business opportunities, open new customer opportunities, and expand into new areas of business?
✓ Have consultants been identified?
✓ Have the strengths, capabilities, assets, and reputations of possible alliance players been developed?
✓ If open discussions proceed, has a contacts list been prepared?
✓ Has legal reviewed all alliance paperwork to ensure the organization is protected and can withdraw without penalty?

> Alliances are a viable alternative to acquiring a competitor to expand business opportunities and customer base. Understanding that there are upsides and downsides to such alliances is critical to the decision-making process. Upon a decision, it is most important to vet the organization and leadership team for possible hidden agendas that could undermine an organization's business goals. Any potential alliance with a foreign organization involves a much more in-depth vetting process and may require government approval.

STRATEGY 24

Know the Competition

When an organization identifies and understands the competition, it has a leg up on developing strategies to remain competitive. Thanks to the world's electronic marketplace, most corporations are acutely aware of their domestic and foreign competitors, or a partnership between both. Depending on the organization's business, it may be prudent to allocate resources to monitor competitor activities, or buy their stock for shareholder information.

Rules

- Develop an understanding of your competitors' product lines and services.
- Monitor competitor marketing campaigns, using social media and other technologies.
- Use competitor technology to improve your organization's goods and/or services.
- Never underestimate the willingness of foreign competitors to use whatever means necessary to beat their US competition, including illicit methods.

Key Points

1. Maintain a process to monitor competitor products, services, technologies, and marketing campaigns.
2. Maintain a process for monitoring foreign competitor products for compliance with US laws regarding safety, quality, and other specifications.
3. Maintain a process to evaluate—and possibly reverse-engineer—competitor products or technology for organizational use.

Discussion

1. Maintain a process to monitor competitor products, services, technologies, and marketing campaigns.

    Use all available media, trade publications, and industry projections to monitor domestic and foreign competitor activities, new product lines and specifications, technology advances, and marketing campaigns. While domestic competitors offer one level of competition in that they play under the same business and government ground rules, Pacific Rim foreign competitors offer a very different and more aggressive level. They can offer the same line of products at a lower cost due to cheaper manufacturing and labor costs even with transportation costs added. Many such manufacturers also have access to various forms of low- or no-cost government financial support.

2. Maintain a process for monitoring foreign competitor products for compliance with US laws regarding safety, quality, and other specifications.

    As stated, it is very difficult to compete with Pacific Rim competitors for reasons listed; however, their unwillingness to incorporate similar US safety laws and guidelines may result in inferior, dangerous products sent to the US. An internal technical assessment could identify such flaws, raise public awareness,

and force the competitor to increase production costs to insure US compliance or withdraw such products from the market.
3. Maintain a process to evaluate—and possibly reverse-engineer—competitor products or technology for organizational use.

- Keeping a means to evaluate and possibly reverse-engineer a competitor's product will provide numerous answers as to their designs, materials, manufacturing, reliability, and limitations. This information might help improve your organization's goods and help prevent over-engineering an otherwise simple design or fabrication.

- Every bit of information that a marketing organization can obtain for a competitor's product is useful in developing marketing strategies for its own product line. From performance specifications to construction materials, warranty coverage to pricing—all can be used against a competitor's products.

Checklist

✓ Have competitor product lines been identified?
✓ Has competitor ownership been identified?
✓ Have product-performance indicators been determined that would raise alarms?
✓ Are competitors using organizational designs or proprietary information?
✓ Have internal evaluations identified product limitations to exploit?
✓ Have internal inspections identified things like new technologies, materials, and packaging that can be incorporated into organizational products?
✓ Have internal assessments found anything about a competitor's product that does not comply with US laws and represents a safety hazard that needs to be reported?

Organizations need to monitor all competitors and competing product lines to identify strategies to combat the competition. They need processes in place to assess competitor products for technical strengths and weaknesses to exploit. World-class products are precisely that: they are the top products in their field and should be exploited to maintain competitiveness.

STRATEGY 25

Understand Snakes, Alligators, and Weasels

It doesn't matter who you are or what position you hold in the organization, there will always be individuals who do not like you for whatever reason. When you come right down to it, these folks are unhappy about everything, and they couldn't care less about those they criticize or target. While most of these are easy to ignore, others can and will do real damage to your reputation and your ability to perform your job. Therefore, it is wise to identify these folks as soon as possible and deal with them accordingly.

Rules

- Identify your snakes, alligators, and weasels as soon as possible.
- Develop a personal strategy for dealing with each type.
- Never underestimate the harm they can do to you personally *and* to the organization.

Key Points

1. How to deal with a snake
2. How to deal with an alligator
3. How to deal with a weasel

Discussion

1. How to deal with a snake

    - A snake can be a friend, confidant, colleague, superior, or direct report. Jealously seems to be a snake's primary motivation. It could be your position, value system, success, leadership style, heritage, who you are, or where you came from that sets the snake off.

    - Snakes will openly support your vision, goals, objectives, and plans for achieving them; but behind closed doors, while feigning support, they will criticize, make fun, offer countersuggestions, mislead, or generate rumors to support their criticisms. They will criticize you and everything that you are trying to accomplish.

    - Nothing is sacred to snakes. They question your intelligence, job knowledge, decisions, motive, relationships, professionalism, communications, timing—anything and everything you hold sacred. They have no integrity or pride.

    - Never underestimate the harm a snake can cause.

        o   A snake will twist facts and speak half-truths to generate distrust, doubt, suspicion, and uncertainty. Snakes dwell in the negative.

        o   It is much harder for a snake to operate in a highly ethical and professional work environment, but snakes find a way.

        o   The amount of energy and time it takes to correct a snake's promotion of misconceptions, rumors, or uncertainty is significant and represents a total waste of time and energy.

    - If you've identified a snake at the leadership or senior management level, quickly remove that individual.

- More often than not, a snake's target is the last one to know. Although the target may have picked up hints here and there, or overheard rumblings, it's hard to believe that a friend and colleague could be responsible.
- When snakes are identified, remove them from their office and the facility using security personnel. Place them on administrative leave until their dismissal is processed. Confiscate all company-issued computers and electronic devices and terminate accesses to data immediately.
- Most employee contracts have legal language that lists unethical and unprofessional behavior as a reason for dismissal. Should an individual not be fired, the problems generated will be extremely costly in regards to wasted energy and man-hours.
- Communicate a statement regarding the dismissal quickly.

• Reassign snakes at lower levels outside the organization or fire them.
- Although a reassignment or warning may work in changing an individual's conduct, it may also result in the person sabotaging computers or taking other devious actions to damage the organization, such as spreading rumors and disinformation among customers.

2. How to deal with an alligator
   • An alligator is visible, open, and usually consistent. An alligator is someone of equal or higher rank who frequently attacks you, your organization, and its processes, functions, activities, and events "for the good of the organization."
   • Alligators are very blatant and open in their criticisms. They will attack anyone.

- Alligators are not stupid. Their attacks may include known or unknown information that could be embarrassing or detrimental to any individual or organization. They may or may not have a hidden agenda. They will frequently make the case or submit a restructuring plan that realigns your organization under theirs or someone else's; reassigns managerial functions to other organizations; or appreciably cuts your operating budget.

- Alligators enjoy the authority of their position and frequently see themselves as power brokers.

- Use the following strategies to deal with an alligator at team meetings:

  o Once you become aware of such individuals' criticism, be professional, courteous, and appreciative of the insight. Use factual information to respond to their observations or criticisms using comparable language. Never show your emotions or get personally offended.

  o If you are blindsided, express your appreciation and advise the team that you will immediately look into the issue and get back to them within a specific time, as the issue may warrant more research. Get consensus from the team that your approach and timetable is acceptable. Report findings at the next team meeting or use emails to communicate your findings. This creates an opportunity to provide additional information to support your approach or identify the underlying reason for the issue.

  o The message you want to send the team is that you are on top of the matter, while allowing yourself to put forward other topics that you want to surface.

3. How to deal with a weasel

    - Every organization has its share of weasels. These are people who are unhappy with their job, the organization, their

- bosses, their coworkers, their pay, their annual rating, their benefits, and their life in general.

- For the most part, weasels are average or better workers and understand the value of complying with organizational policy. Their negativity just makes life miserable for their boss and coworkers.

- Weasels can be tolerated at lower levels within an organization, but they should never be appointed to senior leadership and management levels. Their constant flow of negativity, especially during rough times, can harm the organization far more than any value they may offer or bring to the table.

- The best way to deal with weasels is to maintain good communication flow and a positive attitude throughout the organization.

Checklist

✓ Do leadership communications emphasize the need and value of working as a team?
✓ Do communications stress ethical and professional behavior?
✓ Has an unwritten policy regarding backstabbing been communicated?

> I have dealt, at one time or another, with each of these types. The situations they create are always stressful and require a great deal of wasted energy. Sad to say, these individuals exist in most organizations and at every level within the organization. The bigger the company, the more there are. At the executive level, they can cause a great deal of tension and disruption for their target, their fellow team members, and the organization as a whole.

It is critical that when such attacks happen, the organizational leader host a come-together meeting to openly discuss issues and come to some resolution. The leader cannot allow the negative remarks or observations go unanswered and should answer each allegation with factual data. To do nothing encourages the perpetrator to take the remarks to the next level of dissatisfaction.

This is not about replacing people who simply do not agree. It is about individuals who elect not to accept the direction or consensus of the leadership team and take their criticism and opinions public. A heads-up: it is wise to remember that such negative people have their own circle of friends and supporters.

CONCLUSION

The previous twenty-five strategies offer readers a great deal of information on how to make themselves and their organization more successful. The ultimate goal is to make the organization world-class—one that sets the bar for the entire industry. They are organized to expedite review, understanding, and usefulness. Critical points include the following:

- Take care of yourself and maintain a positive attitude.
    - This is so critical and so full of common sense, yet too many good, hard-working people do not pay attention to the personal challenges that can and will undermine their plans and goals for themselves and the organization.
    - Never stop learning. Take advantage of every opportunity to expand your leadership and management skill sets, to think and plan outside the box, and to learn more about the industry.
    - Give yourself a daily quiet period to relax your mind from the demands of the day or even rethink the day's challenges. This will do wonders in helping you plan new approaches, resolve current issues, and reduce personal stress.
    - Employing various time-management techniques allows you to allocate time and resources to accomplish time-sensitive tasks and strategizing.

- It is not easy to maintain a positive attitude when things are in a downward spiral. Sometimes you have to work at it, knowing that it will have a tremendous impact on personnel in turning things around and getting back on track. Your attitude is one of the most powerful tools you have to energize your team and your entire organization. It can be very contagious.

- Take care of your boss.
    - Your boss is the most important person in your management chain. Bosses can make your business life enjoyable, challenging, and very rewarding. They are in a position to open doors and opportunities you did not know existed.
    - They can also do just the opposite if you do not take the initiative to get to know them on as many levels as possible.

- Take care of your people.
    - There is an old saying that if you take care of your people, they will take care of you. By being a good, fair, and consistent leader, and an effective manager, you can help everyone achieve their own professional and personal goals while taking the organization to the next performance level.
    - Create an environment that keeps your people fully employed, mentally challenged, and safe.

- Take care of the organization.
    - Lead, manage, and set the tone for organizational excellence.
    - Select a leadership team to take the organization to the next success level.
    - Communicate organizational mission, goals, business strategies, and success measures.
    - Set the tone for quality products and service.

- o Implement processes to streamline operations and reduce non-value-added costs.
- o Connect the dots between quality, customer satisfaction, business growth, organizational success, and job security.
- o Celebrate individual and team achievements.
- o Remove incompetent leadership-team members and senior managers.
- o Do not allow unprofessional, unethical, sexist, racist, or other unacceptable behavior to exist.

- Keep the organization informed.
  - o Starting with your boss, your direct reports, and your team members, keep others informed of information that affects them directly or the organization as a whole.
  - o Timely flow of information precludes misinformation, rumors, and a great deal of wasted energy.
  - o Measure everything that is important.
    - the costs of doing business, the organization's overhead, and direct charge rates
    - all overhead costs
    - contract activity, wins, losses, and those closing out
    - staffing requirements and recruiting issues
    - quality initiatives, issues, problems, and statuses
    - customer satisfaction measures, feedback, and statuses
    - program milestones, schedules, budgets, supplier performance, and positive or negative trends
    - research breakthroughs.
  - o Make continuous improvement a way of organizational life.
  - o Use process management to identify and eliminate non-value-added costs for organization operations as well as program-management costs.
  - o Control the number of full-time positions and their compensation.

- o   Seek out veterans who can contribute to the success of the organization.
- o   Develop a series of concise plans that will detail business-expansion initiatives, alliances, contingencies, and emergency responses.

- Enjoy the opportunity to employ every measure of knowledge, experience, and education in making the organization the best it can be—world-class, the standard for other like organizations.

GLOSSARY

These definitions and terms add a little more insight or thinking to the rules and principles discussed throughout the book. This may be the first time they are discussed.

Advanced concepts groups (ACG): Members are tasked to think outside the box to consider and evaluate all possible solutions to a given situation, problem, or issue

Attitude

- *Positive, can-do attitude:* one of the most critical attributes of a leader, manager, or worker for approaching and completing a challenge, task, or job in a qualitative and professional manner on time and within budget.

- *Negative attitude:* one of the least desirable attributes of any individual who spends more time thinking of reasons not to complete a task or job. Workers with a negative attitude frequently provide sloppy inputs that require a redo. Identify and weed out such individuals.

Bosses

- *Outstanding boss:* someone who provides the latitude, resources, advice, and support needed for subordinates to accomplish an assigned job and associated tasks. An outstanding boss is very ethical and straightforward; he or she walks the talk. This individual welcomes input, gives full credit for achievements, and provides quiet or visible support during rough times and protection during difficult times.

- *Good boss:* someone who possesses many of the attributes of the outstanding boss but will occasionally waffle, be indecisive when things are critical, or limit resources or visible support.

- *Bad boss:* someone who is indecisive, political, finger-pointing, and speaks with forked tongue. Bad bosses have no loyalty to anyone other than themselves. When you realize that you have a bad boss, start looking for another job.

- *Terrible boss:* an individual who has no integrity, loyalty, ethics, or sense of responsibility and accountability. Terrible bosses are very quick to blame others for their own incompetence, indecision, or stupidity (includes lying). This individual frequently shouts at or criticizes employees out in the open and is willing to visibly non-comply with organizational policy or procedures. Upon realization that you have a terrible boss, aggressively look for another job.

Communications

- *External:* all official and unofficial communication with customers, the general public, and media. Such communications require proper English without any errors.

- *Internal:* all official and unofficial communication with one or all members of the workforce. This includes website data, written documentation, visual media products, and staff meeting information. Such communications also require proper error-free English.

- *Open-door policy:* a time period during the week that allows anyone to voice concerns or offer suggestions to senior management. Develop a process to outline ground rules for these short appointments. Ideally, individual periods should not extend beyond twenty minutes. These discussions might lead to additional meetings.

- *Open-season survey:* An annual employee survey that asks workers to rate various functions, policies, processes, practices, communication flow, and work environments within the organization. Departments like human resources, finance, travel, security, safety, and facility maintenance should also be rated for responsiveness and professionalism.

Continuous improvement (CI): an approach that encourages all employees to continually look for better ways to do business, and to design, build, and service products while performing their jobs in the most cost-effective, quality-oriented manner possible.

Customer feedback: any feedback the organization receives directly or indirectly from its customers. Customer responses could be in the form of verbal or written communication; a third-party survey; an increase or decrease in sales volume, contracts, or returns; or a break in communications. Implementing a set of matrixes to track all forms of formal and informal feedback to include reasons would help assess areas that warrant attention.

Customer satisfaction: any situation wherein a customer is very happy with a product or service, to include the attention and professional courtesy they received, the quality of the product or service, the warranty and the price, and (if applicable) the delivery, installation, and operating instructions. Periodically surveying key customers could identify strengths and potential issues before they become problems. Anytime there is a problem with a major customer, pick up the phone and call.

Manager

- *Good manager:* an individual designated by the organization who accomplishes the job on schedule and within budget while working with, and through, others to meet performance goals.

- *Superior manager:* an individual who consistently exceeds performance goals and expectations. Superior managers establish a work environment that promotes individual and team success through innovative thinking, empowerment, and growth.

- *Outstanding manager:* an individual who continuously exceeds performance expectations. Outstanding managers create a climate that encourages personnel to seek ways to reduce costs while improving product and service quality, reliability, and customer satisfaction. They frequently performs under-budget and ahead of schedule.

Minimalists: individuals who show up for work and do as little as possible as slowly as possible to draw a paycheck. These persons are the first to say "not my job," whether it is or not. They contribute little or nothing to the organization other than to take up space, and they should be the second group to go in a downsizing mode. Minimalists also enjoy finger-pointing to move responsibility to someone else—unless it is positive feedback, and then they take center stage.

MIS (management information system): the total information technology (IT) or computer system dedicated to the organization or program that holds and processes all organizational information electronically for filing; used as required to run an organization or program. Such systems are frequently compartmentalized with levels of access to ensure that proprietary, program, and customer classified information is protected from unauthorized access or professional hackers. Stand-alone systems offer a higher level of security.

Much more better: a positive increase in any measure; two levels above *better.*

Organization: any level of organization within a larger enterprise or corporation, such as department, directorate, division, branch, group, team, or working group. An organization might be a new initiative, a smaller family business, a major operation, or a multicomponent corporation involving thousands of personnel. This book discusses the basic and advanced skills and knowledge a person should have to lead and manage such an organization. The prerequisite skills cited for such an individual are based on personal experience as a leader and manager in the military, the defense industry, and civil service.

Personal challenges

- *Snakes, alligators, and weasels:* See Strategy 25.

Planning

- *Standard plan format:* an official organization document that includes:
    1. title or subject
    2. scope (applicable to all personnel)
    3. purpose (to communicate near-term business plans or define organization responses to one or more possible natural disasters
    4. responsibilities (who has what responsibilities)
    5. tasks (delineate individual tasks for those responsible)
    6. timelines (identify the timing for actions to be completed)
    7. other (additional information that requires attention).

- *Career planning:* Anyone who takes some time and think about what they want to do and when and where they want to do it will be a winner. We should never assume that the current situation will always remain as it is! A good question to ask ourselves is, "What can I do now to make my current and future situation better?"

- *Contingency planning:* Basically, pre-thinking and documenting responses to possible emergencies, such as natural disasters, accidents, fires, internal or external threats, loss of key personnel, major power outages, and outside hacking. Consider all planning documents to be living things and update as circumstances or events occur or change.

- *Strategic planning:* the discipline of thinking ahead, establishing business milestones for specific accomplishments, and identifying measures that show levels of progress. Such planning is considered mid- to long-term, or five to twenty years.

Prudence: knowing when to keep your mouth shut and thoughts to yourself, know when others are using you to get to others, keeping secrets, and not betraying a confidence, especially ones from your boss.

SME (subject-matter experts): These are individuals who have proven their knowledge, competence, and confidence based on years of experience and hands-on bench/trench level work. They are the go-to folks who know what they are talking about, whether they have one or multiple college degrees or none at all. It could be someone with eons of work experience or some kid or tinkerer who just loves the subject. Find ways to maximize their intellect and energy in solving technical challenges, identifying new approaches, or mentoring other team members.

Stupidity

- Openly criticizing the organization, the leadership team, or your boss.
- Frequent noncompliance with key organizational policies and processes, such as time-card completion or security compliance.
- Frequently using inappropriate language, telling unacceptable jokes or stories, or invading the personal space of the opposite sex.

Thinkers: a very select group of individuals who have a knack for offering good suggestions—a way to create new products and services, fix problems, improve the current product line, expand service, make processes more efficient, build better customer relations, create a more enjoyable working environment, etc. Take time to listen to these folks and find a way to harvest their imagination, energy, and creativity.

80/20 rule: This approach to staffing states that 80 percent of the organization's staffing requirements are designated as full-time positions, while 20 percent of the positions are filled by a combination of part-time, temporary, or independent contractors

ABOUT THE AUTHOR

John Gaston brings forty-plus years of lessons learned from leading and managing a number of nationally recognized organizations within government and industry to the reader. He has led multiple diversely populated intelligence teams—including scientists, engineers, psychologists, physicists, chemists, and human-factors analysts—in assessing strategic foreign aerospace research, development, and test capabilities. He worked with CIA and DIA analysts and decision-makers in elevating national focus on foreign chemical warfare capabilities, Soviet space activities, and advanced aerospace platform designs while orchestrating several successful collection activities.

In Japan and Korea, he supervised teams in operational-intelligence, battle-management, and command-and-control functions. He directed government and industry teams protecting some of the nation's most sensitive, classified research, development, and operational programs, involving thousands of people, hundreds of suppliers, and billions of dollars. During these years, he coached and mentored numerous young officers, civil-service SMEs (subject matter experts), and industrial security specialists in developing their technical, managerial, and leadership skills. Over time, many of these individuals received assignments involving much greater responsibility and authority.

He has lectured at national and international security conferences regarding the need to protect US trade secrets and proprietary information from foreign cyber attacks as well as internal espionage activities. He attributes his professional achievements and accomplishments to the quality, dedication, positive attitude, mission orientation, and self-empowerment of the people he led. Many of his successes were the product of the latitude and flexibility given him by his superiors.

He equates his personal success to his wife and best friend, Maybella.

His awards include Outstanding Civilian Career Service Award, USAF; Special Programs Security Specialist of the Year, USAF/AFMC; C-17 Malcolm Baldrige National Quality Award, Planning Team Member; James S. Cogswell Award, Team Leader, DOD/DIS; Security Education Activity of the Year, Team Leader, SAF/AQ; the Bronze Star medal; three Meritorious Service medals; four Air Force Commendation medals; Viet Nam Honor Medal, 1st Class; multiple USAF organizational awards with "V"; YMCA Golden Triangle Award; and the CYO Eagle of the Cross Award.

.